Erich Fromm

Other titles in Mind Shapers Series

Erich fromm

explorer of the human condition

Annette Thomson

*Open University, the University of the West of Scotland
and the University of Glasgow in Dumfries*

Mind Shapers – Key Psychologists and their impact
Series Editor: Richard Stevens

First published 2009 by
PALGRAVE MACMILLAN

Palgrave Macmillan in the UK is an imprint of Macmillan Publishers Limited, registered in England, company number 785998, of Houndmills, Basingstoke, Hampshire RG21 6XS.

Palgrave Macmillan in the US is a division of St Martin's Press LLC, 175 Fifth Avenue, New York, NY 10010.

Palgrave Macmillan is the global academic imprint of the above companies and has companies and representatives throughout the world.

Palgrave® and Macmillan® are registered trademarks in the United States, the United Kingdom, Europe and other countries

ISBN-13: 978–0–230–51655–7

This book is printed on paper suitable for recycling and made from fully managed and sustained forest sources. Logging, pulping and manufacturing processes are expected to conform to the environmental regulations of the country of origin.

A catalogue record for this book is available from the British Library.

A catalog record for this book is available from the Library of Congress.

10   9   8   7   6   5   4   3   2   1
18   17   16   15   14   13   12   11   10   09

Printed and bound in Great Britain by
CPI Antony Rowe, Chippenham and Eastbourne

Contents

Preface

In writing this book I have approached Erich Fromm's ideas for the third time.

My first encounter with his work was in Germany in the late 1970s, when my friends and I, then in the final years of secondary school, passed round *To Have or To Be?* in the context of a blossoming alternative movement. This book in particular seemed to us to spell out the dawn of a new era which would change fundamentally the way in which we think about society and our part in it.

The second time I came across Fromm was during my studies of psychology in the United Kingdom in the 1980s. While examining different approaches to counselling and relationships I read *The Art of Loving* and was once again inspired by Fromm's clarity and optimism.

My third encounter was prompted by explorations of contemporary social analysis in the UK in the late 1990s. Different writers' views of a society characterized by, for example, 'risk', 'information' or 'knowledge' made me formulate my own ideas, and I began to wonder to what extent long working hours and busy-ness had come to dominate Western societies. Had we become a 'To Do' society? This question made me return to *To Have or To Be?* where I found many ideas highly relevant to what I saw as key features of my contemporary society. Erich Fromm was definitely a writer worth revisiting, as wider and deeper investigation of his work made clear to me. While I had, in the intervening years, developed a more critical approach to some of his views, aided also by two decades of hindsight, I still found his ideas thought-provoking, inspirational and powerful.

This book aims to provide an overview of some key aspects of Fromm's life and his work. It begins with a biographical chapter which gives a sense of how his ideas developed in the context of historically, professionally and personally turbulent times. The following chapters then build up a picture of his analysis of the human situation, his examination and recommendations for personal relationships, his development of humanistic psychoanalysis in therapy, and his investigation and critique of society. The two concluding chapters examine his contributions in the intellectual landscape of related disciplines and in the context of 21st century socio-cultural developments.

This structure means that the book can be read from beginning to end by those readers who would like to gain an overview of these aspects of Fromm's work. However, those who have an interest in a particular field such as therapy or relationships can 'dip into' the particular chapters which deal with their concerns.

Fromm was a writer, psychoanalyst, social critic and political activist of impressive breadth and depth. His attempt to bring together the many strands and contradictions of our existence within a humanistic message of individuality, love and solidarity was exceptional in its scope and applicability. His critique of the *status quo* was acerbic, yet he never seemed to lose a spirit of optimism. There is a strong personal appeal in his writing: if only we think, reflect and analyse, there is still time to change things for the better. This message is reinforced not just in his appeals for better personal relating but also in his calls for social change. Those readers who look for insight and wisdom will find much of this in Erich Fromm's writing. I hope this book will contribute to continued debate and discussion of his ideas, including an exploration of how his thoughts can be taken forward in the future.

Personal Acknowledgements

Many people have provided help and advice with the creation of this book. My thanks go first and foremost to Dr Richard Stevens, editor of this series, for his invaluable insightful guidance, unstinting support and positive presence throughout the journey.

I would also like to thank Dr Rainer Funk, literary executor of the Erich Fromm Estate and Fromm Archive in Tübingen, Germany, for his time, resources and first-hand information about Erich Fromm as a person. Further thanks go to my Palgrave editors Anna van Boxel and Neha Sharma and copyeditor Shirley Tan for their support and advice, to my sister Susanne for practical support in Germany and to Alison, Christine, Janet, Ken and Marguerite for their perceptive comments on draft chapters. Many other friends have supported me in various ways – thank you.

Without the continued patience, encouragement and intellectual and practical support of my husband Norris and my daughters Rosanna and Clara, this project would not have been possible. This book is dedicated to them, and also to the memory of my mother whose lived humanism was an inspiration.

1 A Short Biography

At the height of Erich Fromm's popularity in the United States and Mexico in the 1960s, he received around 30 invitations per month to give lectures and talks.[1] These events attracted huge audiences – for example 2000 students at Chicago University and over 3000 in Mexico City. Some of Fromm's books became international bestsellers and were translated into most major languages. He was seen as a leading figure in a range of academic and therapeutic fields including psychology and psychoanalysis, and a respected spokesperson on a number of social and political issues, from education to nuclear disarmament.

Who was this man whose ideas struck a chord with the hearts and minds of millions of people around the globe and who achieved almost cult status at the peak of his fame?

The eight decades of Fromm's long and productive life (1900–1980) span some of the great political, economic and cultural upheavals of the 20th century. In his work we can trace the influences of a traditional Jewish upbringing in Germany, the First World War, Nazi Germany, and post-war and Cold War years in the USA and Mexico. In his final years in particular he re-developed links to Europe and settled in Switzerland. The strength of his legacy lies in the way in which he analysed the profound social changes of his time and linked them to his view of the human condition. His creative attempts to bring together important ideas from a range of different disciplines make him one of the key thinkers of the last century and also provide highly relevant and stimulating topics for discussion in the present one, as the following chapters will show.

This chapter will highlight several themes in Fromm's life and work. It also introduces briefly Fromm's connections to some of the key figures in psychoanalytic and sociological circles, showing how his theories fit into the rich fabric of ideas and developments in his time.

Fromm was an *enquirer into the human condition*. He addressed some fundamental questions about how we can achieve a meaningful existence, such as how to develop loving relationships and how to build a society which allows us to fulfil our human potential. This led him to a uniquely broad analysis which included the study of religion, philosophy, sociology, psycho-analysis and politics. His was an attempt to explore the diverse influences which shape our lives and to bring together different frameworks of thought in order to make sense of them. Finding answers to his questions was more important than keeping to the artificial boundaries of different disciplines.

He was strongly *committed to autonomy and individuality*. Although he explored and valued the humanistic messages of different traditions of thought in religion and philosophy, he was never a blind follower of any creed, custom or dogma. What mattered to him was the way in which he could grapple with ideas and traditions and then take them forward to new and creative ways of thinking. We can follow in his life the story of a 'stranger', a seeker of truth and meaning, who was never quite settled in any discipline or society. His questioning mind made him a man at home in his ideas and with those who shared them, but kept him at a critical dis-tance from mainstream society and its structures. This is also reflected in his wish not to leave behind the symbols commonly afforded to those who are considered important in society: he was wary of biographies[2] and he did not want a grave; his ashes were scattered on Lago Maggiore.

On a personal level, he showed admiration for people with a genuine commitment to their beliefs. This comes across both in those who could be called his role models and also in his own way of life. It was that quality of personal focus, of integrity and of *congruence between belief and practice* which seemed to stand out in Fromm himself, particularly to those who knew him in his final years. His attempt to learn as much as possible about himself and also about the world around him is demonstrated in his prac-tice of meditation, reflection and self-analysis on the one hand, and his wide interests in the societal concerns of the day on the other. His ability to connect with his audiences and deliver messages of personal meaning to him and to his listeners and readers no doubt contributed to making him such an influential and credible thinker whose ideas came across as deeply held convictions rather than dry erudition or empty slogans.

Childhood and youth – a German Jew

Erich Fromm was born on 23rd March 1900 into the intellectual Jewish community in Frankfurt am Main, Germany. His father, Naphtali Fromm, came from several generations of scholars and tradesmen, going back to his well respected and well known great-grandfather, Seligmann Bär Bamberger (a Jewish scholar in southern Germany). A frequently narrated family anecdote about Bamberger was that he had to keep a small shop to ensure life's necessities but appeared impatient every time a customer entered because it distracted him from his Talmudic studies. The value attached to learning rather than financial gain and the division between study and paid work recur in Fromm's own adult life pattern. He tried to devote each morning to personal study, analysis and meditation and only did paid work in the afternoon. In an interview which he gave in 1974 he acknowledged the influence of his ancestors' values, stating that he found it difficult to accept a world in which the main – and in his view strange – goal appeared to be making money.[3]

A further family anecdote worth mentioning in this context is little Erich's question to an uncle about what he thought would become of him in later life. The uncle's reply was 'an old Jew'. According to Fromm the intention of this remark was to stifle any tendency to pride and ambition. However, this could also be seen as prophetic in the sense that Fromm's life-long striving for understanding, meaning and truth, and his search for integrity, honesty and genuineness may well have had their roots in the intellectual environment of his childhood. They became guiding principles throughout his life – albeit in novel and creative forms, which ultimately meant looking forward to new ways of living rather than back to Talmudic tradition. However, he never lost his fondness for his rich Jewish cultural heritage; its stories and music. Incidentally, Fromm's name means 'pious' in German.

Erich was an only child, in whom a lot of hopes and expectations were invested. His mother, Rosa, was closely attached to her own close-knit family and seemed keen to claim all of Erich's positive characteristics as originating from her side, while the less flattering ones were attributed to his father's. She tried to shape Erich's future according to her own plans. This included, for example, her attempts to make Erich a piano virtuoso à la Paderewski – the famous Polish pianist, politician and prime minister. Fromm described his relief when the detested piano lessons eventually came to an end. His own wish – to play the violin – was never realized. Perhaps the weight of these early expectations stimulated his striving for freedom and autonomy in his later life.

The general atmosphere in the Fromm household appears to have been emotionally charged. Fromm described his mother, a full time housewife, as 'depressive, narcissistic, and possessive',[4] though there is also evidence that she was fond of celebrations and cheerful family gatherings.[5] His father, a wine merchant, seems to have been particularly neurotic and anxious about Erich's well-being. For example, he travelled to Heidelberg to be with Erich for his PhD viva in case it went badly and he might commit suicide. However, Fromm felt that his father was never truly interested in him as an individual in his own right, especially as he grew up. His parents' anxious over-protectiveness of their only child was also one of the reasons why Erich's wish to pursue Talmudic studies in faraway Lithuania never came to fruition.

An important influence on the young Erich's developing identity was Oswald Sussman, a Galician Jew, who was employed in the Fromms' wine business and lived in their household for two years: 'an extremely honest man, courageous, a man of great integrity'.[6] Fromm expresses gratitude and appreciation for the interest he showed in his education, awakening his curiosity about politics and introducing him to socialist ideas. To someone brought up in a close knit traditional community sharing a particular view of the world, these fresh ideas were like a window into a new and exciting one. When Sussman was conscripted at the outbreak of the First World War, the then 14-year-old Erich must have felt a deep sense of personal loss.

Fromm's search for identity is well illustrated in his own assessment of his adolescence:

I was exposed to the same influences as every other young German during this time. But I had to deal with them in my own way. Not only because one always had an exceptional – not necessarily unpleasant – position as a Jew in Germany but also because I felt quite at home neither in the world I lived in, nor in the old world of traditions.[7]

This indicates an awareness of different values and modes of living in his early years. The theme of the *stranger*, of not quite belonging and of alienation played an important part throughout his life.

The young Erich attended the Wöhlerschule in Frankfurt, a boys' school close to his home, with a fairly high proportion of Jewish pupils. He achieved a distinction in his final leaving exam in 1918. His memories of his school years were coloured by events connected to the First World War. He regarded this as a major influence on his personal development, describing his unease when witnessing the displays of overblown nationalism and his sadness over the tragic deaths of individual soldiers he had known personally. These emotions are encapsulated in an event during his English lessons: before the outbreak of the war, the boys had been instructed to learn the British national anthem. When their English teacher asked them to recite this after the war had started, they claimed that this task went against their consciences – motivated partly by naughtiness and partly by the incited hatred against Britain. The English teacher, smiling sardonically, reminded the boys that they should not nourish any illusions: Britain had never yet lost a war. Fromm was profoundly moved by the teacher's calm and rational assessment of the situation, which cut across the irrational wave of nationalistic, narcissistic emotion prevalent in mainstream German society at that time.

He began to ask himself: how is this possible? – a question which he never tired of exploring.

> How is it possible that men stand in the trenches for years and live like animals – and for what? The irrationality of human behavior impressed me in this way, and I became curious about the problem.[8]

This illustrates the adolescent Erich's yearning for understanding, rationality and autonomy, later to become guiding themes in the mature Fromm's thoughts and writings. He returned directly to the 'how is this possible?' question when he formulated his thoughts on and possible solutions to the nuclear threat half a century later. Fromm described the quest for understanding the political and psychological reasons why people go to war as a major thread in his thinking throughout his life.[9]

A further important theme in Erich's adolescent years was his developing interest in the Old Testament prophets, nourished by the Jewish mystic Rabbi Nehemia Anton Nobel, a charismatic preacher who became a central figure to a number of young men in Fromm's circle. Fromm was parti-cularly interested in interpreting the key aspects of the messianic prophets. In his more mature writing he summarizes their main message thus:

> Those who proclaim ideas and at the same time live them we may call prophets. The Old Testament prophets proclaimed the idea that man had to find an answer to his existence, and this answer was the

development of his reason, of his love. They taught that humility and justice were inseparably connected with love and reason.[10]

The prophets also depict visions of messianic time and peace proclaiming 'oneness' and healing, a new accord between people and between humans and nature. However, while the prophets preach of otherworldly harmony, Fromm sees their messages as highly relevant to our human experience. He claims that if we become aware of negative conditions and change our ways, such harmony can be achieved through our realization of human potential.[11]

The deep-seated humanist message which he took from Jewish intellectuals like Rabinkow – with whom he was later to study – began to conflict increasingly with more narrow, Zionist interpretations. After some involvement with Zionist youth organizations, Fromm renounced any Jewish nationalist aspirations. In fact, he became active in campaigning for Palestinian rights in later years.

In his background in the Jewish/German tradition and gradual exposure to different ideas, we can see the young Fromm's attempt to explore tradition yet formulate his own position. His respect for people who live according to their convictions is apparent from these early years and this later became his own quest for himself.

Searching deeper and wider: psychoanalysis and sociology

Fromm's early adult years were characterized by a further searching for understanding and meaning both in traditional and more modern bodies of knowledge. He studied law at the University of Frankfurt and during this time was also involved with the Freies Jüdisches Lehrhaus (Free Jewish Teaching Institute), a Jewish educational centre for adults. A move to Heidelberg University in 1919 opened the door to many new influences yet he also continued with his Talmudic studies. His teacher was the highly respected Rabbi Rabinkow of whom Fromm said that he 'influenced my life more than any other man, perhaps. ... He was a man with whom one could never, even at the first meeting, feel oneself a stranger.'[12] Fromm also developed an initial interest in Buddhism and later became fascinated by this religion which does not rely on the notion of a personal God or on specific religious practices – so utterly different from the Orthodox Judaism of his early years.

He changed his course of studies to sociology and economics and in 1922 completed his PhD thesis under the supervision of Alfred Weber, brother of the famous sociologist Max Weber. The topic of Fromm's thesis was 'the function of Jewish law in maintaining social cohesion in three Diaspora communities'.[13] He examined how a shared belief system operated in holding Jewish communities together, at the same time providing delineation from their wider non-Jewish environment. A beginning interest in the idea of a 'social character' – the notion of a reciprocal effect between social organization and individual psychological processes – is apparent here. These ideas are explored in more depth in Chapters 2 and 5 of this book.

During this time his philosophical studies included the writings of Aristotle, Spinoza and Marx. He was drawn to them because of their pragmatic approach to ethics, viewing people as social beings whose actions have real consequences. Their philosophies address concrete issues: how to live a good life and how to organize society to make this possible. This moral dimension paved the way for Fromm's broad interest in and diverse analysis of the human condition and his role as a respected social commentator who was genuinely interested in the pressing issues of the day.

Encounters with psychoanalysis and sociology played decisive roles in Fromm's adult life. As we will see on the following pages, alliances and disagreements between members of different academic circles had a major influence on the direction of Fromm's life.

During his time in Heidelberg he was influenced intensely by Sigmund Freud's writings on psychoanalysis. Although Fromm never met Freud personally, Freud's approach had a profound effect on Fromm's thinking.

Freud's main concepts were seen as revolutionary in their time, challenging a belief in the self-determining rational individual. One aspect of the Freud's complex model of the person is that of a pleasure seeker whose instincts demand instant gratification. In children we see such calls for wanting things *now* particularly clearly. However, these demands clash with the pressures of social norms embodied in parental discipline. Freud claimed that any unresolved conflicts arising from these opposing pressures are pushed into our unconscious and have a determining effect on our thoughts, feelings and actions, and importantly also our well-being. Repressed conflicts can lead to physical and mental ill health. Healing is only possible through a trained psychoanalyst's interpretation and interventions which allow us to become aware of such patterns and enable us to leave behind the damaging effects their repression may have had.[14]

Fromm's main initial influence in the area of psychoanalysis was Frieda Reichmann, a Jewish psychiatrist 11 years his senior. She became his first analyst, though Fromm moved on to other practitioners when their personal relationship developed. He met her through Golde Ginsburg who was his fiancée for a brief period (though eventually Golde married Leo Löwenthal, Fromm's friend). Frieda Reichmann and Erich Fromm established the Therapeutikum in Heidelberg in 1924. This residential institution was run along the rules of Orthodox Jewish life, reflecting the lifestyles (for example in terms of diet) which both followed. Their approach to treating patients was based on Freudian ideas of repression. Treatment was not limited to patients. Initially, in a kind of bartering arrangement, even the household staff were analysed in return for their work.

Fromm married Reichmann in 1926, though the couple only lived together for a few years. From a psychoanalytic viewpoint, it might well be thought that Fromm's interest in Reichmann reflects unresolved issues in his rather fraught relationship with his mother, given that Reichmann was older than Fromm and initially held a position of authority as his analyst. However, it is also possible that they were brought together by the heady mixture of their initial analyst/patient relationship, their common fascination for Freud's views on the unconscious and their efforts to establish a new institution in the economically volatile climate of hyperinflation in Germany.

Around the time of their marriage, both Frieda and Erich turned their backs on Orthodox Judaism whose rituals they began to see as expressions of unconscious conflicts rather than in themselves meaningful. Striving for harmony in belief and action, they found that orthodox practices which had become empty rituals were no longer tenable: They began to eat leavened bread at Passover. The Therapeutikum project was abandoned in 1928.

An important psychoanalytically orientated influence on Erich Fromm was Georg Groddeck, a doctor and psychoanalyst who ran a sanatorium in Baden-Baden, Germany. Both Reichmann and Fromm had regular friendly contact with him. He was well respected for his astute insights into the relationship between physical symptoms and their psychological basis. Fromm valued him as a man of great kindness and integrity. He put to Fromm the challenging suggestion that the tuberculosis he contracted in 1931, and subsequent need to seek treatment at Davos in Switzerland, was linked to his inability to admit that his marriage to Frieda had failed. Coincidentally, a psychoanalytic view of the causes of tuberculosis had also been the topic of one of Fromm's lectures in 1928. The couple separated but did not divorce till 1940 and maintained a lifelong friendship. Ultimately, Fromm's lung condition was cured by medical rather than psychological intervention.

Fromm took his studies of psychoanalysis further and was himself analysed by different analysts in Munich, Frankfurt, and later in 1928 at the Berlin Institute, where he started his own psychoanalytical practice in 1930. A broad range of seminars and lecture programmes was also on offer there to which a number of famous analysts contributed – including Karen Horney and Wilhelm Reich. This provided a forum for critical discussion of some of Freud's ideas.

Wilhelm Reich's attempts to bring together psychoanalysis and Marxism had a significant influence on Fromm. However, Fromm's ideas part company with Reich's in that the latter retained Freud's strong emphasis on the role of unconscious sexual urges, whose importance Fromm saw as secondary.

Fromm shared Horney's criticisms of Freud's claims about psychosexual development, namely the Oedipus conflict and the father's predominant influence on a child's emotional development.

Freud proposed that erotic drives are present in us from birth and shift in focus to different parts of the body as we mature. Initially, for babies, oral gratification is particularly important. Freud assumed that babies derive pleasure from sucking or biting. This phase is followed by a stage at which the anus is supposed be the area of pleasure. The child learns that he or she has some control over when and where to defecate. Toilet training becomes a potential source of conflict between parental demands for potty training and the child's desire to 'let go' whenever he or she feels like it. For the next stage Freud proposes different developmental paths in boys and girls because the zone of pleasure shifts to their genitals. Freud claimed that the little boy experiences an 'Oedipus conflict'. He is assumed to have erotic feelings towards his mother and experiences his father as a rival. Seeing his father as more powerful and thus fearing him (in particular worrying that the father might castrate him if he found out), he resolves this by identifying with the father and trying to become like him. Freud was less specific about little girls' development but claimed that at the same stage, the girl notices the absence of a penis and fears that she has already been castrated, developing a sense of 'penis envy'. Following a 'latency' phase in which erotic drives are less significant, psychosexual development is concluded in adolescence when the young person develops an erotic interest in members of the opposite sex. However, Freud suggested that the way in which conflicts during the early stages are dealt with can have a lasting effect on our personality, and we can become fixated at a particular stage. For example, the child undergoing strict toilet training may end up becoming a miserly adult intent on holding onto things.

Fromm believed that Freud's views – in particular on the Oedipus conflict – reflected his preoccupation with patriarchal society, omitting the important influence of the mother. The ideas of Johann Jakob Bachofen, a Swiss anthropologist, appeared to address this. Bachofen suggested that pre-historic matriarchal societies emphasizing natural bonds preceded the later development of patriarchal societies in which legal and national principles are particularly highly valued. Social structures of this kind are also reflected in individuals as maternal and paternal tendencies, with the maternal emphasizing family relations, the paternal focusing on duty. Fromm found Bachofen's ideas more helpful than Freud's in showing the importance of both maternal and paternal principles in societies and individuals. In view of his relationship with his parents, Fromm's interest in Bachofen's analysis may not be surprising.

A number of strands can be seen to come together in Fromm's links to a psychoanalytic branch of the Frankfurt Institute for Social Research. Leo Löwenthal, friendly with both Fromm and Max Horkheimer, its director, introduced them to each other. Fromm's work at the institute gave him the opportunity to formulate in more depth his 'grand theory' of social psychology, touching on Marxist sociology on the one hand and Freudian psychoanalysis on the other. Eventually, Fromm received a lifelong contract as the head of the social psychology department. His major piece of work at this time was field research on the lifestyles, attitudes and political behaviour of workers in the Rhineland, exploring the psychological and cultural processes which act as the 'social cement' in these communities. Fromm's thoughts on the effect of the hierarchical structures of unions and political parties were a main impetus for the institute's study of the 'authoritarian character'. He was interested in the interdependent effect of social structure and personal character in an attempt to explain why a number of these workers were drawn towards authoritarianism and fascism.[15] This study will be explored in more depth in Chapter 5.

Not surprisingly, this type of research came under increasing political pressure in the ascending fascist climate in Germany, and the institute moved to Switzerland in 1932, relocating eventually to Columbia University in New York in 1934. Many of its original members followed.

New continents and new visions: the American years

Fromm visited the USA in 1933 as a guest lecturer, following an invitation by Karen Horney. She had emigrated to Chicago in 1932 and was working at the Psychoanalytical Institute there. Horney became an intimate friend and later often accompanied Fromm on his travels in search of a climate favourable for his lung condition. After a further stay in Switzerland for health reasons, he settled in the USA in 1934, following a stream of Jewish intellectuals and others at odds with the Nazi regime for whom life in Germany had become increasingly dangerous.

Believing that Hitler would start a war, Fromm urged his mother (his father had died in 1933) to join him in the USA. She eventually followed his advice in 1939, moving first to Britain, and then finally in 1941 to New York. One of the reasons why Fromm's mother could not join him sooner was financial. Any prospective immigrants to the USA had to provide evidence of financial security. Fromm worked hard in providing this for his mother but was short of $500 which he asked Horkheimer to lend him from institute funds. Horkheimer's reply was negative, though in the end the immigration did go ahead. In New York Rosa Fromm lived a largely independent life, seeking contact with other émigrés. She died there in 1959, aged 83.

There are many reasons for Fromm's estrangement and ultimate resignation from the Institute for Social Research. Having felt let down by Horkheimer regarding his mother's emigration may have been one of them. Fromm's recurring illness may have been another. Further academic and personal differences also played their part.

From the mid-1930s Fromm had begun to question Freudian notions of sexual drives. Freud assumed that sexual instincts play a particularly important part in motivating our actions. Due to society's demands to keep such urges in check, our desires are repressed but remain active at an unconscious level, and psychic conflicts result. Fromm suggested that Freud's theories were reflections of his background in patriarchally organized, sexually repressive societies. Rather than providing 'truths' about humanity in general, they were themselves products of a particular socio-cultural environment. This undermined their claims to universality and questioned their validity in other social contexts. Fromm's attention turned away from sexual instincts as our driving force and he emphasized existential issues instead. According to him, our self-awareness, our sense of aloneness in view of our impending death and our need to relate to others in society are the crucial concerns which shape our psychological development. We will look at this in some detail in Chapter 2.

Fromm's essentially integrative humanistic socio-psychoanalytical approach ran a collision course with several 'orthodoxies'. The combination of his own version of psychoanalysis and sociology was viewed with suspicion. The sociologist Theodor Adorno occupied a more and more dominant position at the Institute and he and Fromm appeared to have disliked one another. Major disagreements arose between Horkheimer (heavily influenced by Adorno, according to Fromm) and Fromm. One serious point of controversy was the role of psychology in the social sciences. Fromm quotes Horkheimer as claiming that 'psychology was only of minor importance for social science anyway'.[16] A second disagreement involved Freud's view on sexuality – his libido theory: Horkheimer dismissed Fromm's and Karen Horney's developments of Freudian theory as 'commonsense psychology', suggesting that 'psychology without libido is no psychology'.[17] The accusation is in itself interesting in that this perhaps explains some of the broad appeal of Fromm's ideas. While the details of psychoanalytic libido theory may seem dry and inaccessible to the lay person, Fromm's approach of bringing together the social and the individual does have a commonsense ring to it. It is clear, accessible and understandable even to those who have not studied psychoanalysis in depth. The criticism could thus perhaps be taken as a compliment (and a reason for massive book sales).

Fromm's relationship with another famous figure of this circle, Herbert Marcuse, was ambivalent, though Fromm appears to have taken Marcuse's work very seriously. A main point of difference between them seems to have been that Marcuse's analysis of society appears to promote regression to infantile pleasures as the ideal. Fromm, on the other hand, emphasizes the importance of our development towards productive and mature relating to others.[18] However, as Burston[19] suggests, we can also see behind such debates a kind of symbolic 'sibling rivalry' among Freud's followers, all vying to become his true heir.

In 1939, coinciding with Adorno's permanent position at the institute, Fromm resigned his life-long contract of employment there. Horkheimer did not follow up or publish Fromm's field data on German workers. Interest in this work re-emerged in later years, and the study was published in Germany in 1980, the year of Fromm's death.[20]

Eventually, a further rift occurred between Fromm and another important figure in his life: Karen Horney. Professionally, they were both involved in two influential circles. One of them included sociologists (among them Margaret Mead and Ruth Benedict) who were interested in cross-cultural research. This provided important material for Fromm's formulation of the link between psyche and society.

A second area of influence was a group of psychoanalysts who shared a strong commitment to humanistic principles. A particularly important figure who had an effect on Fromm's approach to therapy was the American Harry Stack Sullivan. His work on new treatments of schizophrenia was based on the importance of interpersonal relationships and their role in affecting mental health. He questioned the ability of any analyst or doctor to be an impersonal, impartial observer of his or her patients and advocated instead understanding others through warmth and empathy. This was a profoundly humanistic approach which resonated with Fromm's view of relationships and therapy but contrasted sharply with Freud's view of the analyst as more distant and less directive in the therapeutic process.

In 1941, Horney – in conjunction with other psychoanalysts – formed the Association for the Advancement of Psychoanalysis (AAP). Fromm had temporary rights to give clinical seminars there and tried to gain full membership in 1943. This proved difficult because all the other members were medically qualified doctors. Fromm's acceptance would have set a precedent for other non-medically qualified staff – with perhaps a loss of status for the association. However, personal reasons also appear to have played their part. Karen Horney opposed Fromm's acceptance. Their formerly close relationship had become increasingly frosty. Previously, Horney had suggested that Fromm provide training analysis for her daughter Marianne who had completed her medical studies. When conflict developed between mother and daughter, Horney blamed this on Fromm's analysis.

Following Fromm's rejection, several colleagues left the association in protest, and a number of them – along with Fromm – were instrumental in founding a New York branch of the Washington School of Psychiatry in 1943, later to be called the William Alanson White Institute of Psychiatry,

Psychoanalysis and Psychology. The institute had a broad curriculum, edu-
cating psychiatrists, psychologists and also other health professionals in
psychoanalytic principles and general social sciences – an ideal opportunity
for Fromm to bring together his wide interests. Despite his move to Mexico
in 1950, Fromm frequently returned to the institute for annual lectures
and seminars.

From 1939 onwards Fromm wrote and published his work in English.
In 1940 he gained American citizenship and he remained a US citizen even
after his return to Europe. The 1940s generally saw Fromm engaged in a
range of activities, from his psychoanalysis of patients to a full schedule
of lectures and seminars at a number of institutions such as guest lectures
at Columbia University and a teaching contract at Bennington Faculty in
Vermont (1942–1953). These years also established him as an important
writer. Earlier journal articles included papers on psychoanalysis and
Marxism, published in the *Zeitschrift für Sozialforschung,* a journal associated with the Frankfurt Institute for Social Research.

In 1941 Fromm's first book – *Escape from Freedom* – was published in the
USA (UK publication in 1942 as *The Fear of Freedom*[21]) spelling out Fromm's
view of the person, the topic of Chapter 2 of this book. In this seminal
work Fromm describes people as caught in a difficult and far-reaching
dilemma. On the one hand, we experience ourselves as free individuals,
yet we also fear loneliness and isolation. This draws us towards social bonds
with others, with the inherent dangers of being caught up in fascist and
authoritarian groupings, just to escape from – as he puts it – our sense of
alienation:

> the structure of modern society affects man in two ways
> simultaneously: he becomes more independent, self-reliant, and
> critical, and he becomes more isolated, alone, and afraid. The
> understanding of the whole problem of freedom depends on the very
> ability to see both sides of the process.[22]

This is also addressed in his second book, *Man for Himself* (1947) in which
he develops his ideas of a 'social character' and different character orientations, building on Freud's personality theory. Based on observation of
his contemporary society, he argues that a 'marketing orientation' had
become prevalent. This describes the way in which modern capitalist
society produces people whose personalities are judged by what sells best,
who mould and shape themselves to become acceptable to the highest

bidder on the employment market and in personal relationships. Fromm regards these developments as superficial and dangerous because the market becomes the judge of values which are no longer linked to a more meaningful system of morality. Discussion of Fromm's concept of 'character orientation' is included in Chapter 2. Chapter 7 takes this idea further to examine in what ways Fromm's formulation of a character orientation can be applied to the 21st century.

A 'prophet' in his own right? Mexico and return to Europe

For Fromm, the decade of the 1940s was also full of personal developments and challenges. In 1944 he married his second wife, Henny Gurland, a fellow German émigré. Henny's health was poor: she suffered from a type of rheumatoid arthritis, a painful condition for which she received a number of unsuccessful treatments. The Fromms followed medical advice to seek healing or at least a lessening of her painful symptoms at the radioactive springs of San José Purna in Mexico and moved to Mexico City in 1950. This appears to have had only very limited success, and in 1952 death relieved Henny of her constant pain. Seeing his wife in agony for such a long time must have been extremely difficult for Fromm. This perhaps developed further his empathy, strength of character and love of life even in the face of pain and suffering – explored in his later publications like *The Art of Loving* and *To Have or To Be?*. Fromm never had any biological children but maintained a commitment to Henny's son Joseph.

During his long years of residence in Mexico (1950–1973), Fromm still kept up with active teaching commitments at a number of US universities, including a series of lectures at Yale University (Terry Lectures on religion). He was a professor at Michigan State University (from 1957–1961) and from 1962 Adjunct-Professor for Psychology at New York University.

So, why did he stay in Mexico? Given that his reasons for moving there were to do with his second wife's health, a full time return to academic and therapeutic work in the USA may have seemed the obvious course of action. It appears that Mexico provided many opportunities for him to teach psychoanalytic principles there; to be involved in establishing opportunities for students and practitioners to learn about, discuss and develop psychoanalysis without having to worry about squabbles of orthodoxy or personal power struggles. His US teaching activities tended to be more limited to social and political sciences rather than psychoanalysis.

A personal reason was also Fromm's third marriage: in 1953 he married Annis Freeman, a widow from Alabama, who had settled in Mexico. The couple designed and built a house in Cuernavaca, a pleasant colonial city to the south of Mexico City, and moved there in 1956. This reduced to some extent Fromm's involvement in psychoanalytic activities in Mexico City but by no means his creative work. His time in Mexico allowed him to bring together a number of positive aspects in his life: personal happiness in a fulfilling relationship and a beautiful house conducive to writing, meetings and extensive exchanges with friends. He began writing in Spanish.

A further project was the foundation of a psychoanalytic society in Mexico in 1956, the Sociedad Mexicana de Psicoanálisis, supported by a number of colleagues from New York who came to give seminars and lectures.[23] Its aim was to promote a humanistic psychoanalytical approach in psychiatry and psychology, and in medicine more generally. This also included attention to physical well-being and links between body and mind. Charlotte Selver, to whose Sensory Awareness approach Fromm had been introduced by his second wife, was also part of this group.

Fromm's interest in Buddhism was re-awakened. In 1957 he held joint seminars with the then 86-year-old Japanese Zen Buddhist Daisetz T. Suzuki. A particular highlight for Fromm appears to have been Suzuki's meditative practices offering the possibility of deep awareness and involvement in the 'here and now' with its ego-transcending qualities. Again, as a man who practised what he preached, Suzuki seems to have gained much respect in Fromm's eyes.

In 1960 Fromm was able to establish his own version of psychoanalytical training as part of the medical faculty of the Universidad Nacional Autonóma de México, securing close cooperation between the Mexican Psychoanalytical Society and the medical faculty of the university. It included a theoretical course on Fromm's own ideas, entitled 'humanistic psychoanalysis' and a course on 'social psychological phenomena of Mexican culture'. The latter was based on Fromm's analysis of a Mexican farming village, an attempt to study the close links between socio-economic factors and psychological processes in individuals. His student Michael Maccoby was a key contributor to this research. Chapter 2 will outline some aspects of this study.

A new dedicated building was opened on the premises of Copilco University in 1963, and the Sociedad Mexicana de Psicoanálisis changed its name to Instituto Mexicano del Psicoanálisis. As well as training and teaching, therapy was offered there. This was open even to patients who would be unable to afford the often high fees charged by analysts in the US and elsewhere in Mexico.

The balance in his personal life may also have helped to keep together the strands of an extremely busy professional schedule. In an interview with Fromm in preparation for a book on him, Evans observed that he seemed at his most animated when he was able to describe the therapeutic approach he had developed. Fromm's emphasis on maintaining an equilibrium between practical psychotherapy and theoretical writing[24] allowed him to argue from a position of strength in both theoretical and applied issues rarely seen because of the institutional separation of academics and practitioners. It is, however, worth noting that Evans' book was not endorsed by Fromm who suggested that it did not 'give any useful insight into my work'.[25]

In the 1950s and 60s Fromm was engaged in a number of creative projects. The Mexico years provided enough distance from the burgeoning capitalist economies of the USA and Europe for him to develop a more in depth critique of the human fallout of capitalist societies. The theme of the 'stranger' returns. In his typically productive and creative approach, Fromm embraced this in a positive way. It provided him with an opportunity to look beyond the familiar and the obvious and allowed a critical analysis of the situation which he brought back to a core of humanism. Looking back on his life shortly before his death he said: 'Thou shalt love the stranger as thyself. ... One can only understand the stranger fully if one has really been a stranger oneself. Yet to be a stranger means to be at home everywhere in the world.'[26]

In 1955 he published his book *The Sane Society* which includes an analysis of 'humanistic communitarian socialism'. He examines the need for a healthy character orientation to be anchored in institutional structures in society which are sympathetic to our fundamental human needs. For him it was not enough to try to 'cure' the patient: healing had to come from the holistic life situation of the individual. The interdependent nature of individual psyche and institutional and cultural practices comes under the microscope, and he includes recommendations for a healthier society. Soon after publication of this book Fromm joined the US socialist party.

Some years later he resigned, feeling that it had moved too far towards the political right for his membership to remain congruent with his convictions.[27]

His next book, *The Art of Loving,* was published 1956, and it became an international bestseller. In this important work he contrasts unproductive love based on self centred greed with mature productive relationships which acknowledge the individuality of each partner. His ideas were no doubt influenced by his own positive experiences of marriage to Annis. Their relationship appeared to have been characterized by love and companionship, and Fromm valued her comments on his work. This may be a reason why Fromm never returned to writing in German, even after his move to Switzerland.

As well as developing constructive critiques of capitalist societies and their effects on individuals, Fromm continued to grapple with Freud's and Marx's ideas and ways of incorporating them into his own orientation: in 1959 he published *Sigmund Freud's Mission. An Analysis of his Personality and Influence,* followed in 1961 by *Marx's Concept of Man.*

From the early 1960s onwards, Fromm became actively involved in political life, writing about American foreign policy and expressing his increasing concerns about the nuclear threat, for example at a Peace Conference in Moscow in 1962. He was in favour of unilateral disarmament and participated in anti-Vietnam activities. His political involvement took many forms, including petitions to influential groups and figures (among them Pope Paul VI and Bertrand Russell) about concerns in geographically dispersed areas like East Germany, Yugoslavia and Palestine. Growing political activism also appeared to elevate his status and heighten his demand as a speaker.

His attempt to provide analysis as well as vision, and his congruence of theory and life, made him particularly popular with the younger generation in search of solutions to injustice. Hope, optimism and social change were key themes of his approach (for example in *Beyond the Chains of Illusion,* 1962), and he in turn drew strength from his audiences' eagerness to listen to his suggestions. He became a vociferous advocate of his principles of a humanist socialism: an alternative to both Soviet-style communism and Western capitalism.

However, his interest in these developments was not purely political. In the face of the seemingly inescapable march towards nuclear war the old question of 'how is this possible?' returned. How could people remain passive and seemingly unmoved in the face of potential annihilation? He explains this with the suggestion that most people just do not love life enough and links to these tendencies his biophilia (life-loving, positive) versus necrophilia (death-loving, destructive) concepts in *The Heart of Man* published in 1964. *You shall be as Gods* followed in 1965.

His popularity in the US and his political involvement reached their peaks in the mid-1960s. He actively supported Democrat Eugene McCarthy (not to be confused with Joseph McCarthy whose name became synonymous with anti-communist campaigns in the 1940s and 50s) but withdrew from active politics when McCarthy failed to be nominated as a presidential candidate in 1968.

From the late sixties onwards, Fromm's health began to decline: he suffered a heart attack in 1966 and spent time in Switzerland to recover. In 1967 he passed all teaching and training activities to his students who were able to work within well established institutions. Fromm himself intended to devote more time to research and writing. A major project was a comprehensive analysis of human aggression, and he published *The Anatomy of Human Destructiveness* in 1973, an attempt to approach the issue of aggression from a range of disciplines, from anthropology to biology.

From 1969 to 1973 the Fromms only spent the winter months in Mexico, living in Switzerland during the summer. In 1974, after their summer sojourn in their flat in Locarno-Muralto, they decided to remain there. They did not return to Cuernavaca and their affairs in Mexico were settled at a distance.

In 1976 *To Have or To Be?* was published. It became a hugely popular book, particularly in Europe. Examining the writings of thinkers like Meister Eckhart, the medieval Christian mystic, and further key figures in Western and Eastern thought, Fromm takes some traditional messages forward to explore their relevance in the late 20th century. He juxtaposes a productive '*being*' orientation and non-productive '*having*' orientations. For those people who became more and more disillusioned with the pressures of Western capitalism and its potentially destructive competitiveness, Fromm's ideas were like a revelation. They turned him into one of the key figures of the blossoming alternative movements in Europe.

Despite his health problems, the mature Fromm appears to have exuded personal energy and groundedness, making him a charismatic and revered speaker. This is illustrated in the description of how he spontaneously gave a two hour lecture at a Symposium in 1975 which the 400 strong audience followed with complete and untiring attention.

In 1977 and 1978 further heart attacks followed, and the final heart attack on 18th March 1980, five days before what would have been his 80th birthday, brought to an end an extraordinarily rich and creative life.

Death did not spell the end of Fromm's ideas. His best-selling books were reprinted in the years after his death and his influence in a number of areas like psychoanalysis, religious studies, psychology, and sociology continued to attract readers to his works. The establishment of the *International Erich Fromm Society* (with regular meetings and conferences) and an *Erich Fromm Archive* under the leadership of his assistant and fellow psychoanalyst Rainer Funk saw his literary legacy return to Germany (Tübingen) and thus brought Erich Fromm's life story full circle. Funk is also the editor of Fromm's collected works. In 1972 he lived in the Fromm household for six months while writing his own book about Fromm's ideas[28] – *The Courage to be Human.*

In spite of the popularity of Fromm's work, more traditional academic and psychoanalytic circles were at times more wary.[29] This book will

Erich Fromm 1975
Photographer: Müller-May. © Deutsche Verlagsanstalt.

examine Fromm's ideas and influence in more depth. Was his enormous popularity merely an expression of the Zeitgeist of the second half of the 20th century or are there messages which remain meaningful in the context of changing societies in the 21st century?

What we can take forward from this brief synopsis of Erich Fromm's life is a picture of a remarkably creative and interesting man. He was a thinker who did not shy away from the questions central to our human existence, even when the answers appeared to be challenging or difficult. He was also an analyst who approached his patients with humanness and empathy. His striving for moral integrity was an important theme in his own life. For Fromm, psychology could not be a dry 'science', nor could psychoanalysis work without a deep commitment to understanding the person in humanistic terms. Both had to strive towards a holistic view of individual and society from an essentially moral angle. We can think of him as an impassioned explorer of the human condition, whose ideas are well worth taking forward as a springboard for a deeper understanding of our own times.

The following areas of Fromm's work will be examined in subsequent chapters: Chapter 2 will introduce Fromm's view of the person, our existential needs and their implications for the way in which we lead our lives. Chapter 3 will apply these ideas to the context of love in personal relationships, followed by his views on the essential qualities of the therapeutic relationship in Chapter 4. Taking a wider focus on society, Chapter 5 introduces Fromm's social critique and his suggestions for improving society. In Chapter 6 we will examine Fromm's place in the academic landscape of his own time and the present, and finally, in Chapter 7, discuss the relevance of Fromm's ideas in the 21st century.

Overview of Fromm's major publications, life events and wider social and
political developments

Year	Life event	Socio-political developments and events	Publications (Selection)
1900	Erich Pinchas Fromm born in Frankfurt am Main, Germany		
1918	Fromm leaves school and starts law studies in Frankfurt	End of World War I	
1922	Doctorate in sociology from Heidelberg University		
1924	Heidelberg Therapeutikum institution founded	Hyperinflation in Germany	
1926	Marries Frieda Reichmann		
1931	Develops tuberculosis, separation from Frieda		
1932			Publication of article on *The Method and Function of an Analytical Social Psychology*
1934	Emigrates to the USA	Hitler becomes Führer and chancellor of Germany	
1936			Publication of his notion of authoritarian character in Horkheimer's *Studies in Authority and the Family*
1938	Further outbreak of tuberculosis and stay at Davos, Switzerland		
1939		Start of World War II	

Overview of Fromm's major publications, life events and wider social and
political developments – *continued*

Year	Life event	Socio-political developments and events	Publications (Selection)
1940	American citizenship, divorce from Frieda Reichmann		
1941		Pearl Harbour attack – followed by US involvement in World War II	*Escape from Freedom*
1944	Marries Henny Gurland		
1945		End of WWII, Hiroshima attack – first use of atomic bomb in warfare	
1947		Cold War politics, late 1940s to 1950s McCarthyism in the USA: anti-communist campaigns	*Man for Himself*
1950	Move to Mexico City		
1952	Henny Gurland-Fromm dies		
1953	Marries Annis Freeman		
1955			*The Sane Society*
1956	Move to Cuernavaca		*The Art of Loving*
1959			*Sigmund Freud's Mission. An Analysis of his Personality and Influence.*
1961		Building of Berlin Wall, Bay of Pigs invasion and Cuban Missile Crisis	*Marx's Concept of Man*
1962		Peace conference in Moscow	*Beyond the Chains of Illusion*
1964		Vietnam War years	*The Heart of Man*
1966	Fromm suffers his first heart attack	Hippie counter culture years	*You Shall be as Gods*

Overview of Fromm's major publications, life events and wider social and political developments – *continued*

Year	Life event	Socio-political developments and events	Publications (Selection)
1968	Plays active role in Eugene McCarthy's election campaign	Student revolts in Europe, Mexico and USA, Richard Nixon successful in US presidential election campaign	*The Revolution of Hope*
1973			*The Anatomy of Human Destructiveness*
1976	Fromm's health deteriorates: heart attacks in 1977 and 1978	Growth of alternative movement, establishment of Green Party in Germany in the late 1970s	*To Have or To Be?*
1980	Fourth heart attack and death		

2 Fromm's View of 'Man'

One of the compelling aspects of Fromm's exploration of our existence is his ability to bring together many facets of our complex lives. His model of the person takes as a starting point some of our biological givens on the one hand and the existential dilemmas arising from our capacity for awareness on the other. He examines how these are played out in the dynamic interconnection between individual and society, and what implications arise for the way in which we lead our lives.

'Man' or 'Person'?

Fromm tends to use the word 'man' when referring to human beings, and it might be worth prefacing a more detailed examination of his concept of the person with the question of why he uses 'sexist' language, referring to 'man' when he really means 'person' or 'human beings'. The use of the term 'man' in some of his works now seems almost archaic, perhaps even at odds with his humanist principles of equality. This usage was common in his time, of course, and is also related to the lack of an appropriate English term. Fromm himself addresses the issue in his preface to *To Have or To Be?*,[1] written in 1976. He claims that the English language does not have a commonly used word like his native German; 'Mensch' denotes a person of either sex (though it should be noted that its grammatical gender is masculine). Fromm states that he uses 'Man', in capitals, in the more general sense of 'Mensch' in order to avoid difficult circumlocution, justifying this with its traditional usage in humanist writing: an attempt to 'restore its non-sexual meaning ... rather than substituting awkward-sounding words'.[2] Whether this would satisfy feminist objections is debatable. As feminism developed a stronger voice in the 1970s, Fromm began to acknowledge the importance of language in this respect but he certainly did not resolve the problem. No single linguistically elegant solution has been forthcoming since. In this book we will try to avoid rigid categories where possible. Masculine and feminine pronouns will be interspersed in order to counteract any stereotypes.

Human existence: between body and awareness

According to Fromm we are vulnerable and fragile yet also active and creative. Tensions and dilemmas arise from the complex and at times diverging features of our lives. We are anchored in our physical frailties: inhabiting a body linked to time and space, we are born, grow up and mature on a trajectory towards certain death. Illness and pain are often inevitable consequences of our biological reality. At the same time, we possess the great potential of self-awareness and are capable of choice and self-direction. We can develop at least some measure of understanding of our condition: our thoughts can deal with the past, present and future, and we are aware of our own vulnerabilities and finiteness. We realize that nobody else can feel our pain in the same way as we do, and our own death is an inescapable prospect which we each have to face for ourselves.

The development of this self-awareness severed some of our ties with nature and gave us a new and different dimension:

> Man first emerged from the animal world as a freak of nature. Having lost most of the instinctive equipment which regulates the animal's activities, he was more helpless ... than most animals. Yet he had developed a capacity for thought, imagination and self-awareness, which was the basis for transforming nature and himself.[3]

Thus our ability to reflect on life brings with it new needs and challenges, and engenders in us a deeply felt sense of our fundamental aloneness. To avoid the overwhelming feelings of isolation and potential despair arising from this realization, we strive towards some kind of connection with our fellow human beings. Fromm sees this as a fundamental issue affecting every aspect of our lives:

> this awareness ... confronts man with a problem which is essentially human: by being aware of himself as distinct from nature and other people, by being aware ... of death, sickness, ageing, he necessarily

feels his insignificance and smallness in comparison with the universe and all others who are not 'he'. Unless he belonged somewhere, unless his life had some meaning and direction, he would feel like a particle of dust and be overcome by his individual insignificance.[4]

Psychological needs arising from the human condition

According to Fromm, how we deal with the dilemmas of our existence derives from our relatedness to the world. He sees us as primarily social beings who strive to make sense of people and things we encounter in our daily lives. Fromm postulates a negative and a positive option in our attempts to resolve existential dilemmas: we can either regress to 'animal existence',[5] seeking refuge in old certainties, or else we progress towards realization of our human potential. In *The Sane Society*, Fromm illustrates this dichotomy by specifying particularly clearly the different kinds of psychological needs which arise from the dilemmas of our existence – linked to what Allen terms Fromm's 'psychological imperative'.[6]

The first tension which Fromm describes is *relatedness versus narcissism*. The alternatives open to us are to resolve this positively through love and productive relating or else negatively through narcissism, a failure to see the world from another's perspective. Children have to learn to differentiate between themselves and others and gradually develop the ability to appreciate that other people have points of view different from their own. However, if we fail to progress in this way or later lose this ability, we become locked in our own reality, unable to perceive a world beyond ours. In extreme forms this can lead to insanity; milder forms of this narcissism manifest themselves in overblown self importance and failure to acknowledge another person's needs and desires. Developing positive relationships, on the other hand, enables us to square the circle of our existential needs by allowing us to feel unique and independent while simultaneously experiencing a sense of solidarity with other people based on our common humanity. Chapter 3 will explore some of Fromm's ideas on love and productive relating in more depth and detail.

As a second, closely related, need he mentions *transcendence* which addresses how the search for meaning in our lives can lead us to *creativity* or *destructiveness*. Later Freudian psychoanalysis postulates two separate instincts: Eros – life affirming sexuality – and thanatos – a destructive 'death' instinct. However, Fromm sees both as emerging from the same need and he suggests that 'the will to destroy must rise when the will to create cannot be satisfied'.[7] Creativity, Fromm claims, takes us to the positive side in providing us with a sense of happiness and purposefulness.

He develops this notion further in his later book, *The Anatomy of Human Destructiveness*. In his attempt to explore and explain the human propensity to destructiveness from a number of different angles, Fromm includes ideas from psychoanalysis, psychology, neurophysiology, animal behaviour, palaeontology and anthropology. He brings these together in his suggestion that aggression can be categorized as 'benign' or 'malignant'. On the one hand, biologically adaptive life-serving aggression such as defensive aggression can be classed as benign. However, if societies do not nourish our creativity so we can develop productive ways of dealing with our existential needs, negative malignant aggression is the result. It aims at destruction and has no life preserving function.

This links to a further need: *effectiveness*. Once again we can deal with this in very different ways. It can be expressed in the pleasure of contributing positively to relationships, a sense of effectiveness at work or intellectual achievements. If this need is not addressed we run the risk of being overwhelmed by a sense of impotence:

> the sense of being condemned to ineffectiveness ... is one of the most painful and almost intolerable experiences, and man will do almost anything to overcome it, from drugs and work addiction to cruelty and murder.[8]

Fromm also mentions *excitation* and *stimulation* needs in this context, drawing on experimental evidence which shows that even short spells of sensory deprivation lead to negative emotions such as irritability and restlessness.

In *The Sane Society* he claims that these issues are uniquely human: we are the only creatures who can be bored or dissatisfied, and he initially suggests that animals are content if their physiological needs are met.[9] Elsewhere, however, he does acknowledge that restriction of animals' freedom can also result in stifling their potential and lead to destructively aggressive behaviour.[10]

We also experience a need for *rootedness*, a sense of belonging. Negative resolution of this need implies what he calls 'incestuous' clinging to what is familiar. Because we are anxious and fear our own independence we remain part of our narrow traditions without ever contemplating other possibilities. Fromm builds on some aspects of Freudian psychoanalysis here: Freud claimed that we can become fixated at various points of our psychosexual development. However, Fromm sees our *existential insecurity* rather than sexuality as the root of the problem of clinging onto the familiar. We deal with this need positively by developing an outlook of solidarity with our fellow human beings. Rooted and secure in our recognition of the common bond of shared universal humanity, we are then able to develop our own individuality.

A further similar need relates to a sense of *identity*. Fromm suggests that clan identities gave us a stable sense of ourselves in medieval societies and before. When social changes weakened these, new sources for self-definition emerged, such as national, occupational and religious identities. In our attempts to align ourselves to such groupings we run the risk of abandoning our potential for individual freedom in favour of unthinking *'herd conformity'* or blind following of leaders. *Individuality* is highlighted as the positive pole here. Fromm's views on identity have interesting parallels in fellow psychoanalyst Erik Erikson's life-span theory.[11] Contemporary with Fromm, Erikson also developed Freud's ideas and focused on concerns very similar to some of Fromm's. Erikson sees identity as the key issue of adolescence, when young people search for a sense of self and direction. Fromm acknowledges Erikson's work in this area. However, he claims that despite its merits it does not go far enough in investigating this issue in depth. Fromm feels that his own focus on identity as an *existential need* has the edge over Erikson's developmental approach (though clear similarities are obvious in both writers' attempts to account for the experiences of the individual in modern society).

Finally, Fromm also postulates an intellectual and emotional need for a *frame of orientation and devotion* which allows us to find a moral position in the world and a basis for action. This relates in particular to specific belief systems which provide us with a frame of reference and a sense of meaning. Fromm distinguishes between *rational* and *irrational* answers to this. The problem arises here as to which psychospiritual frames of orientation should be seen as Fromm's positive and which as his negative poles.

How are we to decide what is to be classed as rational and what as irrational? He suggests that

> Only the analysis of the various forms of religion can show which answers are better and which are worse solutions to man's quest for meaning and devotion, 'better' or 'worse' always considered from the standpoint of man's nature and his development.[12]

Fromm's own views of religion and faith will be explored in more detail in Chapters 5 and 7.

Orientations to life

How exactly we deal with some of these issues is open to choice, creating in us a tension which we can resolve in different ways. In most of Fromm's writings, he describes a basic alternative with which we are faced. He outlines positive and negative ways of approaching our existential anxieties, based, for example, on Albert Schweitzer's definition of 'reverence for life'. 'Valuable or good is all that which contributes to the greater unfolding of man's specific faculties and furthers life. Negative or bad is everything that strangles life and paralyzes man's activeness.'[13]

Even though we are limited by biological and social factors, we are free to make choices, and these choices are basically between 'good' and 'evil' or 'life and death':

> I believe that man's basic alternative is the choice between life and death. Every act implies this choice. Man is free to make it, but this freedom is a limited one. ... It is man's task to enlarge the margin of freedom, to strengthen the conditions which are conducive to life as against those which are conducive to death. ... Life means constant change, constant birth. Death means cessation of growth, ossification, repetition.[14]

On similar lines, Fromm develops a way of characterizing people in *The Heart of Man*, published in 1964, where he distinguishes between two basic orientations.

The term *biophilia* is the positive pole. Its most basic feature is simply 'love of life'. This is expressed by the person who has developed her human potential and is drawn to happiness and growth. Fromm suggests that family relationships lay the foundations for children's development towards biophilia or its negative counterpart, necrophilia. Stimulation, freedom and positive role models are needed to foster biophilous orientations. He concedes, however, that research in this area is needed to specify the exact conditions in which these tendencies unfold.

In contrast, necrophilia (literally love of death) describes people who are drawn to negativity and decay, who revel in descriptions of illness and death and whose relating to others is characterized by possessiveness, domination and violence. Necrophile people cling to the past, anchored to lifeless objects, and fear the future. Fromm specifies further behaviour patterns such as being drawn to darkness and night. Excessive tidiness and obsession with rules and order are also characteristic for the necrophile person. Not surprisingly, he chooses Hitler and Eichmann as prime examples.

Although Fromm describes these orientations to life in their 'pure' form, he suggests that in reality a mix of both is present in most people. The aim would be to develop as much as we can our biophilous qualities and to create the conditions to make this possible.

The biophilia versus necrophilia distinction also forms the basis for Fromm's social critique, developed further in the 'having' versus 'being' orientations outlined in *To Have or To Be?*. These will be discussed in Chapter 5 in the context of Fromm's view of society.

Character orientations

Fromm also proposes a more specific scheme of analysing and categorizing the habitual ways in which individuals deal with existential needs. In this he sees us as influenced by constitutional factors but shaped significantly by social conditions. He acknowledges the important role the family plays in this process, acting as the agency of society through which norms and values are perpetuated.

In *Man for Himself* (1947) Fromm explicates what he sees as the main *character orientations* and their relationship to society. He states that his descriptions should be regarded as prototypes rather than specific to particular individuals. Most of us incorporate some features of different orientations, with perhaps one or the other more dominant.

On the positive side, dilemmas inherent in our existence can be addressed in a move towards a mature, 'healthy' and productive view of ourselves and others. Loving relatedness and reason are the foundations through which we develop our human potential, the *productive orientation*. This is personified in someone who

> experiences himself as a unique individual entity, and at the same time feels one with his fellow man; who is not subject to irrational authority, and accepts willingly the rational authority of conscience and reason; who is in the process of being born as long as he is alive, and considers the gift of life the most precious chance he has.[15]

In his character descriptions he explicitly acknowledges similarities to Freud's view of personality. Fromm's description of the productive orientation closely resembles Freud's outline of the 'genital character', while most of Fromm's non-productive character orientations find their parallels in Freud's pre-genital personalities. Unlike Freud, however, Fromm does not take sexual drives as the dynamic force which shapes who we become.

As we have seen above, he proposes that it is our relatedness to the world which sets the tone for our character. To explain in more depth how this affects us, he introduces the following notions: *Assimilation* is the term used to describe our relating to objects. *Socialisation* refers to relationships to other people and our view of ourselves.

The first *non-productive* orientation which he mentions in relation to assimilation – our relating to the material world – is the *receptive orientation,* whose defining feature is a belief that all good things come from outside of us. This describes those who passively rely on others to fulfil their needs, whether in the shape of other people or a 'magic helper'.[16] Fromm claims that this orientation can often be found in societies which are organized on the basis of one group exploiting another. Those exploited see their dominators as the source of what they need to survive, believing that their own efforts to change the status quo would only make things worse. This may not seem particularly relevant for Western democracies which pride themselves in having more egalitarian systems. However, he points out that some more covert aspects of the 'receptive orientation' can be found in our belief that 'experts' whose advice we expect to absorb passively can give us the answer to everything from parenting to business success. The economic pressures of consumer society have brought forth 'homo consumens', passive, insatiable, manipulable, always ready to buy into anything that is likely to alleviate his or her underlying fears and boredom.

The *exploitative orientation* describes those people who – similar to those dominant in receptive orientation – also see the source of all good things as external to them but are keen to grab and steal from others. Everybody and everything is judged only on utility value. People in whom the exploitative orientation is central are often characterized by greed and envy. Fromm claims that we can trace the origins of this orientation from medieval feudalism to the plundering of human and material resources in the unregulated free markets of the 18th and 19th centuries.

Also in the 18th and 19th century – along with greater availability of material goods – a *hoarding orientation* took hold. However, this is different from the previous two orientations in that it characterizes those who are focused not on the outside but on their own possessions. This orientation describes people who surround themselves by objects in order to create a sense of security and who feel threatened by the thought of having to give anything away. They often view the past nostalgically and have a sentimental attachment to tradition. People in whom this orientation is dominant come across as miserly and obsessively punctual, and they love order and predictability.

In terms of 'socialisation' – relating to people – these non-productive orientations have their parallels in *symbiotic relating*. This is characterized by an inability to relate to others with individuality and integrity, resulting in negative dependencies. Clinging to others can find active expression in dominance and the corresponding passive version of submission as in sadistic-masochistic relating.

Other non-productive relationships are seen as unhelpful, not because of dependency but because of its very opposite: they are characterized by distance and withdrawal. Fromm regards these as particularly significant in a society in which authorities have become anonymous. This can lead to an *active destructive* orientation characterizing those who are intent on destroying others due to fears that others may want to harm them. In *The Anatomy of Human Destructiveness* he also uses the notion of a *necrophilous-destructive* character orientation to describe psychological developments accompanying the arms race. He sees this as an obsession with lifeless things and violence, which leads to us viewing the world purely in terms of technology and our efforts to control it.[17]

An *indifference* orientation links to specific developments in Western post-World War II capitalist societies and their focus on marketability and advertising – a *marketing character*. In a society in which everything is judged only in terms of its exchange value, regulated by impersonal mechanisms of supply and demand, individuals are alienated from the creative process of work, alienated from their fellow human beings and alienated from themselves. Because we only focus on what sells best we have lost a sense of being centred in the qualities of our own character but instead adapt to the changing winds of what is required by others in a whimsical, opportunistic way. If work necessitates a particular persona, we will dress, behave and 'be' that mask. If we need to be different to please friends in high places, we will do so, chameleon-like, to change to whatever is necessary to 'fit in'. This brings with it a loss of a stable sense of self and of an anchoring in our own values.

As we will see in Chapter 5, this is also a key feature of Fromm's social critique. It is worth noting that Fromm raised these concerns as early as 1947 when – in comparison to the marketing pressures of the present time – consumerism was in its infancy.

In his later writings he also used the term *narcissistic orientation*[18] as a character description to alert us that our distance from others can also show itself in our inability to appreciate that there are realities beyond our own. We (as individuals or social groups) are the only gauge of what is seen as appropriate and are hypersensitive to any kind of criticism, however justified. Our distance from others manifests itself in us losing ourselves in our own self-centredness.

Fromm, it seems, was a humorous man who enjoyed telling jokes to illustrate his points. As an example of a mild – and rather common – form of this orientation, he recounts the following joke: A narcissistic 'writer meets a friend and tells him in great detail about what has been going on in his life. Finally he says: "Enough about me – let's talk about *you*. How did you like my latest book?"'[19] Interestingly Fromm described himself (and also Freud) as having 'narcissistic' tendencies.[20] Schecter remembers the elderly Fromm pondering over 'how one's own narcissism is the most difficult trait to overcome'.[21]

The character orientations outlined here are theoretical descriptions. In reality, Fromm claims, we embody different tendencies in various mixtures, and nobody is completely productive or entirely non-productive. Even generally non-productive characters can have positive traits. However, overall orientation can affect how they come across. For example, in someone of generally productive orientation, hoarding traits can appear as 'patient' or 'careful', while this mix within an overall non-productive orientation would manifest as someone who is 'lethargic' or 'anxious'.[22]

Such character schemes do not only apply to individuals. Fromm also suggests that we can analyse *societies* in terms of the predominant orientations which are characteristic at a particular time and in a particular place. Claiming that we can specify a *social character* which describes similarities shared between members of the same culture in terms of how they relate to the world, he defines this as:

> the nucleus of the character structure which is shared by most members of the same culture in contradistinction to the individual character in which people belonging to the same culture differ from each other.[23]

Empirical study of 'social character'

What evidence is there to support such a schematic approach to our relatedness to the world? Together with his colleague Michael Maccoby, Fromm used these notions as the basis for empirical research. Their aim was to examine and analyse the character orientations of Mexican villagers at a time of profound social change from traditional farming communities to consumer societies. The study was also supported by numerous members of the Mexican psychoanalytic society who initially gave their time without being paid.[24]

The team used the following methods: a questionnaire covered over 80 questions about demographic information and lifestyle. It also included items about respondents' views on various social and political topics from parenting to world peace. Questionnaire replies were supplemented by descriptions of dreams and projective methods, such as the Rorschach Test in which the respondent explains what images he sees in an inkblot. This is interpreted to gain insights into unconscious processes.

Fromm and Maccoby provide a detailed account of how these questionnaires were scored to allow them to identify particular constellations of character orientations. Their results of the mathematical technique of factor analysis provides some evidence that particular character traits do indeed group together in the way envisaged in Fromm's descriptions. Findings regarding character constellations were related to various other sociological variables to give an account of, for example, what types of orientations were prevalent in different social classes.

The study provides a fascinating picture of a particular culture, with details about views on healthcare, schooling and work as well as personal fears and hopes. To give an example of their approach we will focus here on one specific aspect of the study: alcoholism, affecting around 15% of men in the village.[25] Based on interviews and observation, those who were seen as unable to work for several days each week due to their drinking habits were classed as 'alcoholic'.

The researchers explore the impact of cultural, economic, social and psychological factors which can be related to alcoholism. We will examine briefly the psychological aspects they propose. They note a connection between a passive-receptive character orientation and alcoholism. Those classed as 'alcoholics' were more likely to show indications of personal powerlessness in relationships and beliefs in a magic solution to life's problems. Further, strong regressive mother-fixations were more likely in 'alcoholics'.[26] The researchers speculate that alcohol was used as a way of overcoming a sense of personal impotence. An orientation which was *less* common in 'alcoholics' was the 'hoarding' tendency. Conversely this was more commonly found in teetotallers.

The researchers suggest that individual character orientations interact with social changes. Due to their fixations on old securities, those with passive-receptive orientations remain rooted in outdated notions of a traditional patriarchal farming society. With the decline of these structures due to increasing industrialization, new ways of deriving personal power and connection needed to be found. People whose character orientations did not incline them towards saving and valuing material goods felt powerless in the context of a competitive materialistic society. Their receptive orientation made them more likely to seek quick, short term solutions to their insecurities and they turned to alcohol.

While this research provides a detailed picture of a particular culture at a particular time, such links are, of course, problematic. For example, we could question if it is really the case that a 'passive-receptive' orientation makes alcohol abuse more likely. Could it be, for example, that those classed as 'alcoholics' have developed the feelings of powerlessness indicative of 'passive-receptive' orientations as a result of their addiction? Further research would be needed here, in particular studies which trace an individual's character orientations and lifestyles throughout life.

Freedom and relatedness: the development of the individual

In more general terms, Fromm believes that our lives ultimately follow a path of increasing fulfilment of our human potential: *individuation and freedom*. This is the case for us individually (ontogenetically), in the child growing into an adult, and as a species (phylogenetically). Both as individuals and as a species we move beyond the constraints of our early stages and face the challenge of finding *productive forms of relating* with our fellow humans in complex modern societies.

Ontogenetically, children leave behind the (in most cases) soothing closeness of family and home environment and have to find their own paths towards becoming their own persons. This development is accompanied by a growing sense of separateness and isolation from their primary influences. For the developing child, physical, emotional and mental development lead to increasing self-strength whose limits are partly set by 'individual conditions but essentially by social conditions.... The other aspect of the process of individuation is *growing aloneness*.'[27]

Where initially those primary ties, the familiar and safe environment of home and family, provide a sense of security and ward off a sense of isolation, adolescents increasingly have to find their own answers; freedom and individuation bring with them the need to develop new frames of orientation on an individual basis:

> Once the stage of complete individuation is reached and the individual is free from these primary ties, he is confronted with a new task: to orient and root himself in the world and to find security in other ways than those which were characteristic of his preindividualistic existence.[28]

This search can be supported by the process of *psychoanalysis* in which the analyst, like a mountain guide, points the individual to the right path and gives him or her the courage and support to keep going. Fromm felt that access to psychoanalysis and encouragement to engage in self-analysis and self-reflection should be available to all, regardless of income or mental health status, a tool in the 'art of living' rather than purely a treatment for those seen as mentally ill or unstable.[29]

Fromm claims universal, culture-free validity for his view of the mentally healthy person:

> ...[the] concept of mental health follows from the very conditions of human existence, and it is the same for man in all ages and all cultures. *Mental health is characterized by the ability to love and to create, by the emergence from incestuous ties to clan and soil, by a sense of identity based on one's experience of self as the subject and agent of one's powers, by*

the grasp of reality inside and outside of ourselves, that is, by the development of objectivity and reason.[30]

The rational, creative and loving individual emerges as Fromm's ideal of a balanced person who has realized his or her potential. He seeks to bolster his claims by pointing out that 'This concept of mental health coincides essentially with the norms postulated by the great spiritual teachers of the human race.'[31]

Fromm's student, co-researcher and colleague Michael Maccoby states that Fromm's view was that 'the self was like a mansion of many rooms in which most people lived in one or two with the others closed off'.[32] The aim, then, would be to explore hitherto unknown riches and examine what stops us from accessing them, even if our lives will never be long enough to allow us to explore all nooks and crannies.

Chapter 4 will provide a more detailed account of Fromm's approach to psychoanalysis and his views on the way in which therapeutic encounters can help us to grow towards what he sees as the fully developed person.

Freedom and relatedness: the development of humanity

Our path towards freedom and positive relating to others can also be traced in our phylogenetic development: 'the history of man can be characterized as a process of growing individuation and growing freedom'.[33] Fromm regards this freedom as an essential aspect of our existence. Its origins lie in two interrelated evolutionary developments: first, he points out that for those creatures 'higher …in animal evolution' there are fewer instincts which predetermine behaviour in a simple, predictable cause and effect way. In humans, he suggests, 'the force of instinctual determinism moves toward the zero end of the scale'.[34] In parallel, the evolution of an enlarged neocortex made flexible learning and behaviour patterns possible and paved the way for awareness, language and imagination. In psychological terms, the absence of an instinctual basis for behaviour has created a vacuum: flexible behaviour and thought patterns became possible but this also brought choice over how to behave, how to lead our lives and how to find a consistent basis for moral judgements.

Fromm likens this development to the biblical story of Adam and Eve who were expelled from paradise once they tasted the apple of knowledge. Their choice of ignoring God's command not to eat the fruit represents an essential turning point in our history: the development of self-awareness means that our essential unity with nature was broken. In his analysis of this story, Fromm points out that going against God's commands is regarded as a sin by establishment churches but can be seen as 'the first act of freedom, that is the first *human* act.'[35]

Fromm highlights that the result of Adam's and Eve's expulsion from paradise was suffering; gone was the comfort of a conflict-free life in which everything was provided. This parallels the psychological suffering inherent in our awareness of our aloneness and finiteness and our search for new ways of relating. He uses this as an illustration of the distinction between 'freedom from' and positive 'freedom to': Man 'is free *from* the sweet bondage of paradise but he is not free *to* govern himself, to realize his individuality'.[36] Freedom is possible but we often turn away from it. Choice and responsibility can lead to anxiety and doubt and we sometimes find it easier just to hand over decisions – and thus also our freedom – to others. The converse is Fromm's notion of *positive freedom* based on 'the principle that there is no higher power than this unique individual self, that man is the centre and purpose of his life'.[37] Living itself becomes the ultimate meaning of life.

In evolutionary terms, the freedom to make choices and develop our capacities is the beginning of a long process. The transformations made possible by self-awareness and creativity are obviously enormous – tool use, language, art and industrialization – not to mention the possibility of profound reflection about the nature of our existence itself. Fromm marvelled at these developments: 'I believe that the development of man in the last four thousand years of history is truly awe-inspiring.'[38]

The other, darker, side of this development is our sense of isolation and vulnerability. Just as the apple of knowledge led to Adam and Eve becoming aware of their nakedness in the biblical story, self-awareness took us away from nature: as far as we know, we are the only animals who are aware of our limits and vulnerabilities quite as clearly and explicitly. Despite this potential split of our being part of nature and yet apart from it, Fromm does not see nature and culture as separate systems. In fact, he regards our physical shortcomings as the starting point for our cultural development. His view of our biological nature in relation to culture is one of interdependence, or rather, perhaps, in some ways a paradox: '*man's biological weakness is the condition of human culture. ...* He invents tools and, while thus mastering nature, he separates himself from it more and more.'[39] Some of these formulations can also be seen as astute observations relating to the environmental problems facing us today.[40] Technology has brought huge benefits and has allowed us to overcome our limitations in many ways: we can fly, use computers and drive our cars to the nearest supermarket but at the same time our impact on nature changes it and creates conditions which in turn threaten our survival and produce further social, psychological and technological problems.

Fromm proposes a historical and developmental view of the answers which different societies have given to our need for relatedness. As the earliest and oldest way of dealing with our existential awareness, he charts an attempt to regain relatedness with nature. He claims evidence for this from the rites of the so-called 'primitive' religions which often emphasize nature gods and goddesses; the earth mother. Fromm regards these ways of remaining related to nature and home cult as regressive, deficient and not conducive to maximal utilization of our powers of self-awareness:

> By remaining bound to nature, to mother or father, man indeed succeeds in feeling at home in the world, but he pays a tremendous price for this security, that of submission, dependence, and a blockage to the full development of his reason and of his capacity to love.[41]

The creation of positive bonds with our fellow human beings is crucial and Wilde[42] rightly identifies solidarity as a key theme in Fromm's view of our essence. Fromm describes the core issue of positive relating as follows:

> There is only one possible, productive solution for the relationship of individualized man with the world: his active solidarity with all men and his spontaneous activity, love and work, which unite him again with the world, not by primary ties but as a free and independent individual.[43]

Historically, more sophisticated solutions gradually emerged, once economic and social conditions freed up time and energy for reflection. As cultures became more complex, Fromm suggests that further significant shifts can be observed between 'the middle of the second millennium B.C. to the middle of the first millennium'.[44] During this period, some of the major world religions developed, all sharing the belief that the solution to our existential dilemmas lies not in regression to unity with nature but in trying to realize our human potential. The basic principles of solidarity and love are the ideals which link them.

> All norms of the great humanist religions like Buddhism, Judaism, Christianity, or Islam or the great humanist philosophers from the preSocratics to contemporary thinkers are the specific elaboration of this general principle of values. Overcoming one's greed, love for one's neighbor, knowledge of the truth (different from the uncritical knowledge of facts) are the goals common to all humanist philosophical and religious systems of the West and the East.[45]

In an age in which religion is often seen as the antithesis to scientific truth, it may come as a surprise to see Fromm link these frameworks under the heading of 'truth' seeking. However, if we see 'truth' as an articulation of the values which Fromm views as linked to the essence of our existence and a new way of relatedness, we can appreciate – even if not necessarily accept – his argument.

It is important to clarify Fromm's views on the history of *ideals* and *ideologies* in this context. He hails the development of humanistic values as progress. However, he highlights that they were abused by those in power for their nefarious purposes of oppression through ideologies, resulting in distortions of the very ideals that underlie them. A difficulty here might be to define what is seen as an ideal and what is regarded as ideology. This is easier to do with extreme examples and the benefit of hindsight. While we have no problems in viewing the actions of the Catholic Church during the Inquisition as fundamentally anti-humanist and thus also against the teachings of Jesus, we still struggle with the details of exactly how to translate the ideals of religious masters into action in our complex world.

Rejecting the accusation that his vision simply mirrors subjective preferences Fromm invokes the usefulness of these values:

> It is a solution which has been experienced by many individuals and also by groups, religious or secular, which were and are able to develop the bonds of solidarity together with unrestricted individuality and independence.[46]

Fromm asserts the validity of his argument by suggesting that only positive relating to others allows us to develop our individuality yet at the same time remain connected to others – a theme which is developed in more depth in Chapter 3:

> This is the reason why the solution of brotherliness is not one of subjective preference. It is the only one which satisfies the two needs of man: to be closely related and at the same time to be free, to be part of a whole and to be independent.[47]

Transforming lives

As discussed here and also shown in Chapter 1, Fromm was a respected psychoanalyst, writer and social commentator, well known for his astute assessment of patients as well as the social ills of his day. His aim was not just to understand individuals and society but to promote more positive and productive ways of relating at all levels. While Fromm's examination of the individual and his social critique often point to negative ways which we have developed for coping with our anxieties, he is generally optimistic about the possibility of us developing conditions more conducive to a productive resolution of our dilemmas.

Fromm describes this with characteristic passion in *The Revolution of Hope*:

> Man and society are resurrected every moment in the act of hope and of faith in the here and now; every act of love, of awareness, of compassion is resurrection; every act of sloth, of greed, of selfishness is death. Every moment existence confronts us with the alternatives of resurrection or death; every moment we give an answer. The answer lies not in what we say or think, but in what we are, how we act, where we are moving.[48]

In this sense, Fromm's message is clearly a *moral* one, not only scrutinizing problems but also outlining solutions and providing life guidance. Working with the assumption that it is possible to specify what our human needs are and under what conditions we flourish, he proposes ways forward for productive development of the individual and for the social change needed to make this more achievable.

In establishing clear-cut statements about the universality of the nature of our existence and how to live productively in keeping with our human needs, Fromm is bold in his assertions of certainty. His views are far removed from some current postmodern thinking in the social sciences. This approach emphasizes the social and cultural relativity of values and calls into question any universal claims about our selves and needs. Fromm, on the other hand, is keen to articulate the commonality of our human experience. Frie,[49] for example, points to the fundamental difference between Fromm's conceptualization of the person and the postmodern view which challenges the notion that we have a 'core self' and thus also questions the possibility of specifying universal conditions of human existence. However, overly relativistic accounts which deny any universality of experience run the risk of avoiding any direct statements about how we *should* act. This is perhaps especially problematic for psychology itself, a discipline to which many people turn for life guidance.

For similar reasons Fromm also distances himself from Sartre's existentialism whose focus on the supremacy of personal freedom and denial of any 'valid, objective values'[50] he saw as an expression of unconstructive despair and egoism. Furthermore, he asserts that Sartre's ideas were lacking a systematic clinical evidence base.

Fromm suggests that psychology cannot turn its back on moral issues. On the contrary, he feels that the discipline has a duty to provide the basis needed for specifying valid norms of productive living in society.[51]

Ingleby asserts that Fromm's ideas – in particular his social critique – are highly topical in our times yet not fashionable in some academic and political spheres because of the suspicions directed at any approach which assumes a 'right' and 'wrong'.[52] Fromm himself regarded such attempts to evade moral questions as a stumbling block to creative and innovative thinking:

> Another … way of discouraging original thinking is to regard all truth as relative. Truth is made out to be a metaphysical concept, and if anyone speaks out about wanting to discover the truth he is thought backward by the 'progressive' thinkers of our age. Truth is declared to be an entirely subjective matter, almost a matter of taste.[53]

In contrast to the position Fromm denigrates here, his own approach is openly moral and political, providing what he saw as much needed life guidance at the level of the individual and society.

The origins of Fromm's ideas

Having taken a brief look at some aspects of Fromm's concept of the person, it is important to set some of his ideas into context. Fromm was an avid reader who was deeply interested in both current social developments and older sources of inspiration. Funk observes that 'Fromm definitely spent infinitely more time reading than writing (perhaps twenty or thirty times as much)'.[54]

Fromm's humanistic view of the person is a theme which runs across all of his writing. It can be seen as his life's work to articulate what he regarded as the nature of our existence, the challenges arising from our very being in the world and the ways in which these should be met. As shown here and in the previous chapter, his approach to understanding the nature of lived experience is broad. At a theoretical level it is based on his wide knowledge and exploration of some of the principles of Judeo-Christianity as well as Eastern religions such as Buddhism, and brings together some of their ideas with those of thinkers like Aristotle, Spinoza, Goethe, Marx and Freud to flow into a 'grand theory' of the essence of our existence and development.

Here are just a few very brief examples of influences on Fromm's thinking. The Old Testament prophets and their call for people to awake and mend their ways provided inspiration for the urgency of his message for personal and social change. From the New Testament Fromm took on some of Jesus's ideas on love and solidarity. From Buddhism, he followed messages on 'mindfulness of being'. Aristotlean ethics inspired some of his views on how to live a virtuous life in a community context. Spinoza guided some of his thoughts on the search for meaning beyond the notion of a personal God. Goethe provided ideas on humanism. From Marx he took on the importance of economic relations and the need for an action orientated philosophy. A very important source of influence was, of course, Freudian psychoanalysis. While Marx's ideas alert us to the need to become aware of and change our social circumstances, the same could be said about Freud's views of the individual. It is through psychoanalysis that we learn about our unconscious conflicts, and this process also offers us the opportunity to reflect, change and move forward. Fromm was also impressed by the notion of 'reverence for life'[55] put forward by Albert Schweitzer, his contemporary. These influences, together with his experiences of German,

American and Mexican societies provided a rich font of ideas on which Fromm could build his view of the person.

Thus the label 'grand' fits his approach both in terms of the breadth of traditions and views on which his ideas are based as well as its scope for application: his theory covers the historical development of the human species as well as the chronology of individuals' life paths; it can be applied to personal issues as well as to relationships and an analysis of society.

If his comes across as a rather ambitious mission, Fromm is positive and optimistic about the possibility of reaching some clear conclusions:

> I believe that man's essence is ascertainable. ... The essence of man consists in the ... contradiction inherent in his existence, and this contradiction forces him to react in order to find a solution. ... By the very fact of his being human, he is asked a question by life: how to overcome the split between himself and the world outside of him in order to arrive at the experience of unity and oneness with his fellow man and with nature.[56]

While we can recognize the importance and urgency which Fromm accords to these issues, claims like: 'Man has to answer this question every moment of his life'[57] may initially come across as rather inflated; many of us ponder the existential issues which Fromm rightly proposes as essential but such concerns may not be a preoccupation in the way suggested here. Then again, Fromm's view is that we develop positive or negative orientations towards life in general. In this sense he certainly has a point in highlighting that our answers to the dilemmas of our existence are not just isolated philosophical deliberations. They affect how we think, feel and act.

Evaluating Fromm's view of the person

What, then, should we make of Fromm's view of 'Man'? Tauber suggests that by

> combining a clinical wisdom secured through almost 50 years of intensive psychoanalytic experience with a life-long devotion to humanistic studies, Fromm ... has fashioned a conceptual formula-

tion of man's nature which is unique and classical in its vigor and simplicity.[58]

This could be seen as an astute assessment of much of Fromm's work. Directness and lucidity are hallmarks of his conceptualization of the nature of our existence. However, to what extent the simplicity of some of his formulations is a strength in its clarity or a weakness in its bordering on the simplistic is open to debate, as will be discussed below.

As we have seen, Fromm's intense interest in literature, religion and philosophy gave him a vast reservoir of ideas. He also maintained an openness and curiosity in disciplines bordering his own. At the same time he worked intensely with a number of patients in a psychoanalytic context and gathered clinical experience, though not in a statistical or strictly 'scientific' way. While he provided some empirical studies of his notion of a 'social character', most of his ideas are based on rather general – albeit astute – observation.

Those readers who are looking for a scientific basis to his claims will find many of Fromm's assertions too general and unsubstantiated. If psychology is to be regarded as a science which should aspire to testability and statistical evidence, many of Fromm's ideas would be seen to be in urgent need of further scrutiny, at best starting points for further scientific enquiry. Many of them appear to be built on his observations in a fairly general sense, translating into psychological terms a diverse array of some of his favourite religious and philosophical principles.

We can argue back, of course, that he did address this in his attempt to express his ideas in statistical form in his Mexican study. However, even there, controversy remains regarding his choice of methods. We can question to what extent questionnaires, projective tests and dream analysis can be taken as reliable evidence of underlying character structures.

On the other hand, others may consider the foundations on which Fromm's ideas are built as strong in wisdom and experience. To those seeking inspiration and life guidance, Fromm's ideas have a lot to commend themselves. They can be seen as an insightful merging of different strands of theorizing about the human condition. Religious moral advice couched in psychological terms may well have filled a particularly important niche in the American and European post-war world of dwindling congregations disaffected with establishment churches yet in need of moral guidance from other sources.

This could perhaps also explain some of the recent renewed interest in Fromm's work. In times of uncertainty, bold claims – even if not all of them turn out to be accurate or practicable – may seem preferable to moral vagueness, a point developed in more depth in Chapters 6 and 7. Re-examination of Fromm's view of the paradoxes of our existence and the psychological and social implications arising from these could be timely in the midst of our own period of social change.

Even if we leave aside questions regarding Fromm's evidence base, criticisms of the notions of individual and societal character orientations can be raised. While Fromm himself specifies that 'character' describes certain constants across situations and tries to give a distinction between situational responses and deeper character structure we can still question how meaningful such 'character labels' are. At times they come across as rather circular: 'the biophilous, life-loving person will decide for biophilous values, and the necrophilous person for necrophilous ones'.[59] The good person chooses good values, the bad person chooses bad values – yet how do we know who is biophilous rather than necrophilous other than by their values? Rather than seeing his character orientations as accurate ways of describing others, they may give us more of an indication of where Fromm himself was coming from, an insight into his own view of the world.

Furthermore, some of the specifics of Fromm's categorization of non-productive traits into negative or positive come across as rather arbitrary. For example, the dividing line between 'self-assured' (seen as positive) and 'arrogant' (negative)[60] could be difficult to discern and is very likely to depend on the perceptions of the observer.

With regards to Fromm's productive character orientation, Schaar also makes an interesting point. He suggests that Fromm's ideal leads to an image of someone who lives life for life's sake, pleasant and amiable but not consumed by passion or involved in heroic deeds. It appears to convey a bland sense of self-satisfaction in the demeanour of the enlightened: 'the face of productive man is empty. It lacks character.'[61] We might argue, however, that amiable blandness may be preferable to destructive passion.

Another point to question is his characteristic formulation of extremes set against one another. Might there be a tendency to oversimplify complexity when we juxtapose productive with unproductive relating, biophilia with necrophilia, and 'productive' with 'non-productive' character orientations? Such stark categorizations serve a useful function in alerting us to the basic differences in these orientations but may run the risk of over simplistic and perhaps even prejudiced pigeonholing.

After all, Fromm himself pointed to the dangers of prejudice and stereotype: 'I believe that one of the most disastrous mistakes in individual and social life consists in being caught in stereotyped alternatives of thinking.'[62] This seems a rather surprising statement from the writer who explored the human condition with such dichotomous terms as biophilia versus necrophilia or the 'having' versus the 'being' orientations. However, it is also important to view some of these dichotomies not as simplistic alternatives but as dialectic, representing the pull in opposite directions and the dynamic tension between two poles.

The strength of Fromm's dualistic expressions lies in their clarity. Their dangers come from the temptation to take his ideas simplistically to characterize the 'enlightened': those who choose 'life', show biophilous tendencies and develop towards individuation, as against the developmental philistines who follow the crowd. In reality, such distinctions may hide a number of complexities. The road to the development of our potential, however we describe this, may be rather more complex than the impression one could get from some of Fromm's ideas. As Schaar suggests: 'Fromm's work is full of these incompatibles. ... As a consequence, his work is tense and vigorous, full of movement and dare. As another consequence, any reader can find just about what he looks for in Fromm.'[63] His clear 'one-or-the-other' formulations have undoubtedly made his work accessible and popular and have in this sense contributed to his main purpose: to alert us to the need to be more aware of the essence of our existence and its challenges. Their strength as conceptual tools is not to be dismissed.

What are we to make of Fromm's view of personal autonomy and tradition? Why does he see a following of traditional thought and value systems as regressive and irrational? Would a child remaining within the comfort zone of her familiar way of life not make a rational decision in remaining where she grew up and following the same values and traditions? This would suggest that only individuals turning away from tradition would seem to be able to develop their full potential – a bold claim. In view of Fromm's own break with a number of dogmas and traditions this assertion is perhaps not surprising.

However, this raises some difficult questions for Fromm's own thinking, too. After all, the major justification for some of Fromm's ideas comes from traditional thought systems. Do they not also constitute 'herd following' rather than individuality albeit of a more select, humanistic kind? The counter argument here would be that a carefully considered choice to take on particular ideas would be very different from blind following of thought frameworks whose aims and purposes have never been questioned.

We can read into Fromm's analysis of our existential needs his own struggle with uncertainty, insecurity and aloneness in his life: the challenges brought about by his memories of growing up during the first World War years, the rise of the Nazi regime, moves from Europe to the USA then to Mexico and finally back to Europe, drifting apart from his first wife and then his second wife's death. It would seem surprising if the deeply reflective Fromm had not included some of these themes in his analysis. The challenges in his own life may have brought home to him the dark side of rootlessness particularly strongly. However, while Fromm was, of course, a man of his own time, we are indeed all touched by the issues he raises.

As we have seen, there may be circularities in some of his definitions. There may also be areas which may prompt more questions than they answer. We may disagree with some of the strong claims he makes and take on a more cautious stance. Still, Fromm's ideas have a lot to commend themselves through the sheer compelling nature of their main arguments. Few writers have managed to bring together so many aspects of our lives, paying attention to individual, interpersonal and social consequences of the paradox set by our existence. The awareness of our vulnerable embodiment and the inevitability of death cause at least some measure of anxiety in the vast majority of us. How we deal with the dilemmas arising from these issues individually and socially is thus certainly a concern with wide appeal. Fromm rises to the challenge by giving us a thought-provoking analysis of what he sees as the fundamental essence of the nature of Man and its implications for our lives.

3 Loving – A Special Art?

In a book about Fromm, a chapter on love and relationships deserves a special place, since his passionate commitment to love shines through his writings on many topics. According to the testimonies of people who knew him personally, it was also a key feature in his own relationships. He was clearly a master of this art, as can be seen in Funk's and Maccoby's descriptions of intense, lively and energizing encounters with Fromm. Funk recalls that:

> Whenever I wanted to more fully comprehend what Fromm actually means by 'productivity', 'reason and love as [one's] own powers', 'biophilia', or the 'being mode of existence', I found it helpful to recall the effects of the face-to-face encounters with him.[1]

Similarly, his supervisee and friend Rose Spiegel describes his 'talent for intimacy'.[2]

Love played a significant role in his own experience. Fromm's life story shows that he had some painful lessons to learn and could take neither love nor life for granted. There is nothing like loss or the fear of impending loss to make us appreciate what is important to us. His serious illness (tuberculosis in 1931) as well as having to fear for his own and his family's safety in Nazi Germany must have been stark reminders of the fragility of human life. When his second wife, Henny Gurland, became ill, his devotion to and care for her seem to have been exceptional and moving. The years of living with Henny's intense pain yet being unable to relieve her suffering must have tested Fromm's emotional powers to the limit. After Henny's death, Fromm appears to have undergone a fundamental change, battling with feelings of powerlessness and despair, and no doubt also loneliness.[3]

He was able to move on from these dark emotions to transform them in a new relationship. However, the theme of the fragility of life continued. Both he and his third wife, Annis Freeman, had to deal with life threatening conditions. Annis developed cancer in the 1950s. She recovered after an operation and followed – together with Fromm – a strict diet to prevent recurrence.[4] Fromm himself also had to battle with further ill health; he suffered his first heart attack in 1966. The bond between him and his third wife appears to have been particularly intense and loving. Observers in the 1970s describe moving displays of obvious affection between the elderly couple.[5]

These personal experiences may have made Fromm value life, relationships and love with such intensity. His existential lessons were acquired through bitter experience, and perhaps the way in which he was able to turn this into his characteristic optimism in his own life makes his ideas all the more credible.

Ideals of loving: mature love versus symbiotic unions

In *The Art of Loving,* published in 1956, the central place which he gives to love in human relating is set out particularly explicitly. As so often in Fromm's work, clearly structured accessible writing makes his ideas easy to follow. One factor which may have contributed to this is that he noted down his ideas on a particular topic as far as possible in one sitting.[6] *The Art of Loving*, a bestseller in its heyday and translated into many languages, expresses his views on the fundamental importance of love and compassion in human relationships and has provided inspiration for many people around the globe. His theoretical ideas come across as interesting and carefully thought out, his practical suggestions as generally reasonable.

As we have seen in Chapter 2, Fromm suggests that our awareness of our own finiteness can make us feel lost and alone. The unease provoked by our sense of isolation, he claims, is the 'source of all anxiety'.[7] He regards this as a fundamental issue, more profound than history and culture: 'The deepest need of man … is the need to overcome his separateness, to leave the prison of his aloneness.'[8] Fromm's overall solution to our existential anxiety is unequivocal. He calls *love* the answer to the problem of human existence. 'This desire for interpersonal fusion is the most powerful striving in man.'[9] Or: 'There is only one passion which satisfies man's need to unite himself with the world, and to acquire at the same time a sense of integrity and individuality, and this is *love*.'[10]

These statements suggest that he had discovered meaning in his own life and was keen to pass on this important message. Whether we take these ideas as polemic or inspirational will, of course, depend on our own values and visions. Fromm clearly took a strong stance on the significance of interpersonal relationships.

In *The Art of Loving* he develops ways of making sense of relationships and brings in the contrasting positions of *symbiotic* and *mature* unions. He suggests that *symbiotic* unions can be either passive (characterized by submission or masochism) or active (based on domination or sadism) but both types share the same feature in that neither partner is independent and does not approach the relationship with a sense of individual integrity. The bond is based on mutual need and dependence rather than a secure sense of self which each partner brings to the relationship. This idea is developed further in *To Have or To Be?* where he suggests that unions which are built on 'possessing' or greedily controlling another person in the 'having' mode leave a relationship fraught with conflict and jealousy. *Productive, mature love*, on the other hand, allows us to overcome our sense of separateness but we still retain our integrity and individuality without the unproductive dependence involved in symbiotic relationships.

Fromm outlines a number of features of mature relationships: for example, the importance of *giving* in the sense of giving of oneself. When we share our understanding and emotions, this means that in the recipient, too, a sense of aliveness is engendered. Thus, Fromm suggests, 'Giving implies to make the other person a giver also and they both share in the joy of what they have brought to life.'[11]

Some of these ideas are closely related to the concept of the *'productive character'* (see Chapter 2) which regards giving as a way of expressing aliveness and joy. He illustrates this in what he calls the most 'elementary' example: sexuality – the way in which a couple mutually give of themselves and of their love. He associates this active giving with both men and women: while in sex the man may seem to be the more obvious 'giver', women are equally seen as giving of themselves, both in intercourse and ultimately through motherhood. According to Fromm, active giving is also expressed in care and tenderness: love is the concern for growth and development in those we love. 'Where this active concern is lacking, there is no love.'[12] 'One loves that for which one labours, and one labours for that which one loves.'[13]

As we have seen in Chapter 2, Fromm views the active, rational individual as the ideal of the productive character. With regards to relationships he also emphasizes the notion of 'will': 'To love somebody is not just a strong feeling – it is a decision, it is a judgement, it is a promise.'[14]

The skills of love

For those who aspire to this type of relating, Fromm provides inspiring guidance as to how we might work on the qualities and skills needed for love. However, Fromm warns the reader of *The Art of Loving* not to expect any prescriptions. While his aim is to specify some of the 'premises of the art of loving',[15] the actual experience of it needs to be practised and worked on by each person for him- or herself.

Fromm argues that we need to recognize love as an 'art': something which we cherish for its own sake, something about which we can reflect on a theoretical basis and, perhaps most importantly, something which we must practise in order to achieve mastery. Just like with other art forms, we need to focus on aspects of practice which may seem peripheral to the end product (much like a musician learning scales before being able to play a piano concerto). As part of this practice he specifies three essential skills which indirectly contribute to our learning the art of loving.

The first of these is *discipline*. In modern societies, Fromm suggests, we find this difficult because our lives are tightly regulated between work routines and the demand for 'laziness' when we are not on duty. With our leisure time dominated by the desire to do whatever we want in an attempt to escape the demands of imposed authority, we lack the self-imposed rational discipline necessary to avoid chaotic and fragmented lives. In line with Fromm's own life pattern of regular time set aside for self-reflection and meditation, he recommends getting up at regular hours, devoting regular amounts of daily time to cultural and physical activities (music, good books, walking, meditation), avoiding overindulgence in relation to food and drink and limiting time spent in 'escapist activities like mystery stories and movies'.[16]

Furthermore, he argues that 'discipline should not be practiced like a rule imposed on oneself from the outside, but that it becomes an expression of one's own will'.[17] Thus the emphasis is on self-discipline and the rules of a healthy lifestyle. In support of this, Fromm appeals to Eastern thinking and its long tradition in recognizing 'that that which is good for man – for his body and for his soul – must also be agreeable, even though at the beginning some resistance must be overcome'.[18]

Such ideas link to Fromm's notion of a *humanistic conscience* which he claims does *not* represent the internalization of external authorities and notions of duty. It is instead connected to our sense of integrity and care for self development, and guides us towards actions based on these values.[19] However, the noise of modern life and our concomitant inability to spend time alone in self-reflection militates against us listening to the voice of conscience. If we ignore this, we experience a sense of discomfort, which can even lead to mental or physical illness. As we have seen in Chapter 1, Fromm had a longstanding interest in the interaction between physiological and mental well-being. (As he got older his assessment became rather more pragmatic, illustrated in his suggestion that 'one could believe all illness was psychosomatic until you reached your 60s, then you had to accept the fact that the body wears out'.[20])

A second necessary condition for practising love is specified as *concentration*. Fromm gives concrete suggestions for concentration practice: sitting still for at least twenty minutes twice a day without any distractions such as 'reading, listening to the radio, smoking or drinking' to allow full awareness of 'being', free from intrusive thoughts about past events or future plans. Concentration also involves developing sensitivity to ourselves; recognition of our psychological states and reasons for them. We develop this, he suggests, from our ability to 'be open to our own inner voice which will tell us ... why we are anxious, depressed, irritated'.[22]

Furthermore, Fromm advocates the practice of concentration on *all* our tasks; giving full attention to whatever it is we are doing at a particular moment – also an essential aspect of listening. He recommends the practice of this type of concentration in particular to people who love each other. This involves giving full attention to the other person rather than thinking of what we want to say or do next.

Fromm claims that we find it difficult to achieve this level of concentration in our culture amidst the bustle of our busy daily lives. Being comfortable with our own company and achieving stillness are rare qualities. We can regard this as an especially important message for our times when this type of concentration is often undermined by the pressures of a competitive society which squeeze out time for personal development and relating in work and private spheres. These tendencies will be discussed in more depth in Chapter 7.

His third factor, *patience,* like the other two, also goes against the fast and relentless pace of his (and our) times. Our economic system of maximizing profit nourishes notions of speed at work and in transport. According to Fromm this militates against the very qualities needed for building the basis for loving relationships.

As well as giving advice on what we *should* do (the practice of concentration, discipline and patience), Fromm tells us in no uncertain terms what we should avoid. He suggests, for example, that trivial talk – 'conversation which is not genuine'[22] – chatting for the sake of it while our heart is not really in it, is not conducive to discipline or love. In a strong and judgemental tone he suggests that we should steer clear of bad influences (by which he means people with negative and destructive outlooks or 'the company of zombies … whose soul is dead'[23]). At the very least we should deal with such people in a more positive transformational way by challenging clichéd talk and not getting drawn into further negative trivialities.

Qualities underpinning mature love

So, how can the skills of discipline, concentration and patience be developed? Fromm suggests that we need to focus on particular qualities in our approach to love, too. One example is *objectivity.* This seems a rather odd feature to highlight in the context of love. Fromm defines objectivity as the opposite of narcissism. In narcissistic relating we are only able to see others in relation to ourselves rather than for who or what they are in their own individuality. For example, a child is seen as a credit to her parents, a husband as useless because he fails to conform to his wife's image of perfection. What Fromm means by this objectivity is an ability to 'see people and things *as they are*, objectively, and to be able to separate this *objective* picture from a picture which is formed by one's desires and fears'.[24] Rather pessimistically, he regards 'objectivity' as the exception, and claims that 'a greater or lesser degree of narcissistic distortion is the rule'.[25]

However, a suggestion to see people 'as they are' carries its own challenges and problems. Two observers may well see the same person in different ways. How do we judge in whom 'objectivity' resides? In Fromm's terms, 'objectivity' means taking a thoughtful approach and developing an awareness of our own motives, desires and weaknesses. It implies a measure of being honest with ourselves when we examine our relationships with others.

Objectivity depends on a further two qualities, all prerequisites for love. In terms of our thought processes he calls our ability to think objectively *reason*. Related to our emotional stance towards objectivity he suggests that an attitude of *humility* is essential. This entails an absence of narcissism in the sense that we do not see ourselves as the centre of the universe and are able to develop a realistic picture of ourselves, having 'emerged from the dreams of omniscience and omnipotence which one has as a child'.[26]

Fromm argues that love, objectivity and humility are indivisible. Once we have developed these capacities, our lives take on loving orientations towards ourselves and others, family and stranger. Although personal relating is the obvious locus where love is expressed, Fromm highlights the close connection between the individual, personal relationships and wider circles: 'if I truly love one person I love all persons, I love the world, I love life'.[27] 'Love for one person implies love for man as such.'[28] He claims that 'If someone would want to reserve his objectivity for the loved person, and think he can dispense with it in his relationship to the rest of the world, he will soon discover that he fails both here and there.'[29] This serves as a reminder of Fromm's view of love as an orientation towards one's whole life, from personal relating to wider political issues.

Another ingredient is to have *faith* in the other person 'to be certain of the reliability and unchangeability of his fundamental attitudes, of the core of his personality, of his love'.[30] He clarifies that this does not mean naïve assumptions of someone standing still and staying the same for ever but a conviction that his fundamental stance towards life is a part of himself and will not alter. (However, it is worth noting that Fromm generally did not suggest that people cannot change, and worked with the assumption that fundamental transformation is possible. The most striking example of this is perhaps his assessment of the character orientation of Albert Speer, a key figure in Hitler's Nazi destruction machinery. In the post-war years, following close scrutiny of Speer's life story, his letters and dreams during his imprisonment, Fromm concluded that a destructive character can indeed change.[31])

A further quality is *courage*; by this he means that we should be ready to take risks and accept disappointment rather than be held back by a fearful avoidance of pain. *Activity* is also involved in love, according to Fromm, and he highlights the importance of a sense of aliveness and curiosity: 'The capacity of love demands a state of intensity, awakeness, enhanced vitality, which can only be the result of a productive and active orientation in many other spheres of life.'[32]

Fromm brings *The Art of Loving* to an interesting conclusion: He ends what initially appears to be a focus on interpersonal relations by branching out to two different spheres: first, the *personal* – the importance of each person developing within herself the characteristics and qualities which Fromm regards as prerequisites to love. He also moves onto the *societal domain* in suggesting that:

> Those who are seriously concerned with love as the only rational answer to the problem of human existence must, then, arrive at the conclusion that important and radical changes in our social structure are necessary, if love is to become a social and not a highly individualistic, marginal phenomenon.[33]

With this, he sets the scene for further exploration of how social conditions can be created which are sympathetic to the development of a loving orientation. This will be outlined below and is also one of the areas discussed in more detail in Chapter 5.

Types of love

As we have seen above, Fromm sees loving as a general orientation to life and puts forward generalized qualities and skills conducive to our capacity for productive relating. However, he also presents an analysis of five different *types of love*.

Brotherly love

He sees the humanistic solidarity underlying what he calls brotherly love as the foundation for all kinds of love. This type of love is characterized by equality upon which an edifice of care and compassion is built. It is an inclusive type of relationship and implies union and solidarity. Its basis is a fundamental experience of humanness; loving each other in our frailty which is part of the human condition. We are all at some point the givers or receivers of compassion: 'we are all in need of help. Today I, tomorrow you.'[34] This loving of our sister or brother in 'the stranger' is the fundamental quality which we need to develop. What is particularly refreshing and touching in his account is the sense of true humanistic equality which underpins Fromm's description. There is no paternalistic, patronizing call to help 'the less fortunate' from a position of superiority: we all share the fundamental frailty of being human, and, importantly, we also share with others our strengths and our autonomy.

Schultz poignantly describes how he and many other people who came into contact with Fromm were touched by his deeply held humanistic beliefs: 'The realisation of the universality of our fragile existences can help us develop a sense of solidarity with all living creatures and move us to a sense of empathy and caring.'[35]

Motherly love

The next type of relationship which Fromm examines is motherly love. He makes a fundamental distinction between the main characteristics of maternal and paternal love. Motherly love stands for unconditional love 'no matter what', whereas fatherly love represents conditional love, dependent on the degree to which the child is seen to fulfil expectation and duty. To guard against stereotypical expectations, Fromm points out that these need to be seen as general attitudes rather than prescriptions for specific individuals. Not all fathers always follow the principles of paternal love in their interactions with their children just as not all mothers express maternal, unconditional love all the time. He highlights the importance of balance between paternal and maternal principles to avoid the excesses of harsh judgement on the one hand and of loss of judgement on the other.

In this analysis he draws on Bachofen's anthropological account of matriarchal and patriarchal principles and the way in which these can operate in individuals and societies: the paternal contains the positive aspects of reason and discipline but negative potential of hierarchy and oppression. The maternal, in contrast, has on its positive side a life affirming sense of freedom and equality but can be negative by manifesting itself as regressive: tied to the apron strings of clan and soil, we are unable to develop a sense of individuality and reason.

Fromm chooses to focus on motherly love for a more detailed analysis in this context, because he sees in the relationship between mother and child the beginnings of a loving orientation *per se*. This love is based not only on fulfilling the infant's needs but also on affirming the child herself and instilling in her love of life itself. Research in developmental psychology confirms some of these points in suggesting that the nature of attachment styles between mothers and their children can indeed set the tone for later relationships.[36]

In contrast to brotherly love, maternal love relies on a much more unequal relationship in which the mother appears to be all-giving and the helpless infant the permanent receiver of her attention and care. Perhaps tellingly in the light of his own childhood experiences Fromm suggests that ultimately the loving mother needs to be able to support separation, letting her child move along his own path, and, importantly, still to keep on loving. This, he claims, she can only do if she is centred in her own self. According to Fromm, even this type of perhaps seemingly more exclusive relationship ripples into wider circles in that the loving mother will also show concern for children in a more general sense, a desire to nurture the helpless and share love with others.

Erotic love

Fromm describes erotic love as exclusive; however only in the sense that full and intense 'fusion'[37] is achieved with only one person. Fromm's idea of mature erotic love implies that 'it loves in the other person all of mankind, all that is alive'.[38] He contrasts this with more illusory types of love: examples of this are erotic 'love' resulting from possessive attachment or based exclusively on sexual desire. Such desire in itself, he suggests, can be stimulated for a number of reasons, love being only one of them. It can also be motivated by 'the wish to conquer or be conquered, by vanity, by the wish to hurt or even to destroy'.[39] He claims that the quality of tenderness, linked to a sense of 'brotherly' equality and respect, is what distinguishes the deeper kind of love through which separateness can be resolved from the unproductive orgiastic type of union (outlined below).

To the 21st century reader this may sound rather old fashioned and idealistic. However, when these points are seen in their context, it becomes clear that Fromm strives towards an interesting synthesis in his acknowledgement of some paradoxical aspects of human relating. In the sense in which we can all be seen as one, as equal (as in 'brotherly' love), fundamental existential aspects of the human condition are indeed shared. On the other hand we are also all unique individuals, and linked to this 'erotic love requires certain specific, highly individual elements which exist between some people but not between all'.[40]

Male-female relating

Fromm's ideas strongly contradict more traditional psychodynamic Freudian views which postulate an instinctually driven basis to love, in particular erotic love.

Fromm describes instinct theory more generally as 'the straight-jacket of orthodox psychoanalytic theory...which...slowed down the further development of the understanding of man's passions'.[41] He believes that the focus on instinctual drives – and particularly Freud's emphasis on sexuality or *libido* – actually detracted from an understanding of the issues of real importance to both Freud and Fromm: the nature of our emotions, of love and hate, the way in which they can lead to conflict and unhappiness in human relationships, and, according to Fromm, how they relate to our existential needs.

Fromm describes Freud's view as a misunderstanding of the essence of love. He suggests that Freud was wrong in 'seeing in love exclusively the expression – or a sublimation – of the sexual instinct, rather than recognizing that the sexual desire is one manifestation of the need for love and union'.[42] In fact, he goes as far as accusing Freud of not understanding sex deeply enough. Fromm's emphasis is firmly on the quality of relating rather than the achievement of libido gratification and he highlights the importance of moving psychoanalysis from its focus on the biological to a more existential realm.

Furthermore, Fromm claims that Freud seriously misunderstood the nature of both feminine and masculine aspects of character and sexual function. He sees Freud's views as linked to the outdated notions of patriarchy from which they arose. This made Freud analyse sexuality from a predominantly masculine perspective, and female sexuality was largely ignored. Fromm criticizes Freud's notions that boys experience women as castrated men while women suffer from 'penis envy'. According to Fromm, *relationships*, not biological drives, help to shape who we become. His assessment of Freud's view on love and sexuality is epitomised in his interpretation of one of Freud's dreams in which he (Freud) sees, displayed in a herbarium, a dried flower. Fromm interprets the flower as a symbol for love and sexuality. Instead of focusing on the creative aliveness of these emotions, Freud attempted to study them in a scientific, cold and distant way.[43] Alternatively, or perhaps additionally, this may also reflect the lack of sexuality in Freud's own marriage, with the dried flower the memory of past pleasures now out of reach.[44]

Fromm suggests that some differences between men and women derive from different functions in sexual relating. Men tend to emphasize achievement and ambition, with anxiety relating to failure to perform. For women, on the other hand, attractiveness and dependency are more significant concerns, with fears centred on loss of beauty. However, while Fromm relates such tendencies to 'natural' differences based on sexuality, he emphasizes that these patterns are now much more closely related to societal norms and economic pressures. Dependency as a feature of women's psyches, and ambition as a part of men's orientations, are more likely to be a result of patriarchal economic structures. He is also at pains to distance himself from any stark categorizations and compares differences between the genders to musical keys which provide an overall tone but do not in any way determine specific tunes. Because men and women are above all human, sharing the same existential fears and needs for relatedness, it is more important to emphasize their commonalities.

He also dissociates himself from some of the thinking of his time which in his view implied that equality means sameness. According to Fromm, male and female polarities complement one another in mature love. Fromm sees attraction of 'opposite poles' as a key feature of sexual union both biologically and psychologically. He regards this polarity between the masculine and the feminine as the basis for creativity, in the obvious sense in biological reproduction but also in the psychological sense: 'in the love between man and woman, each of them is reborn'.[45] He also emphasizes that in individual men and women both masculine and feminine forms of relating are present: 'Just as physiologically man and woman each have hormones of the opposite sex, they are bisexual also in the psychological sense.'[46] He attempts to support this rather speculative leap from biological to psychological arguments by linking it to polarities in nature (for example darkness and light) and their poetic descriptions in Eastern literature.

Same sex loving

What happens if this polarity is not biologically apparent, as, for example, in same sex couples? In *The Art of Loving*, Fromm deals with homosexuality in a rather brief passage and describes this 'deviation' as '…failure to attain this polarised union', with the consequence that 'the homosexual suffers from the pain of never-resolved separateness, a failure, however, which he shares with the average heterosexual who cannot love'.[47] This is perhaps an area where Fromm shows himself to be a man of his time. Some of the joyful images of same sex couples celebrating their official unions in Britain in 2006 seem to communicate genuine commitment and care rather than failure. We might apply to Fromm the comment he made about Freud: fifty years on, sexual mores have changed. Thus, in this respect Fromm's views – like Freud's – need to be seen in their particular cultural context, which casts doubts over some of his claims to universal validity.

On the other hand, Fromm can also be seen as ahead of his time in some ways: in an article entitled the *Changing Concepts of Homosexuality in Psychoanalysis* (published in 1940)[48] Fromm explicitly refers to changing social norms and an increasing tolerance of homosexuality in society, in particular vis-à-vis gay women. In contrast to Freud, he highlights the importance of considering the details of personal and not just sexual relating. Homosexuality as such can thus have positive or negative aspects depending on how each individual deals with the relationship. Fromm claims that for those with homosexual tendencies the social stigma they encounter is often the main problem. In 1970, in a letter to a young man who contacted him with a concern about his attraction to other men, Fromm suggests that he would be well advised to reflect on and analyse his own feelings beyond the fear of others' reactions. Highlighting that homosexuality should not be seen as a malign symptom he points out that there may be more homosexuals than heterosexuals who are capable of love. Ultimately, however, he describes homosexuality as a 'limiting' factor in life.[49]

Self-love

In his exploration of *self-love* Fromm outlines first of all the importance of delineating this from narcissism. This distinction is particularly important since self-love is seen in such a negative light in some aspects of the Judaeo-Christian traditions. He points out that 'Selfishness is not identical with self-love but with its very opposite'[50] and highlights that self-love and love of others should in no way be seen as mutually exclusive. Genuine love of oneself, he suggests, is rooted in the same concern and striving for development and growth as forms of 'other'-love. In accepting the equality of all human beings 'I', also human, need to show the same respect and care for myself that I demonstrate towards others: we need to root the origin of life affirming qualities such as happiness, growth and freedom in love for ourselves. Selfish people, in contrast, display a generally less respectful attitude towards life and themselves, often based on emptiness and frustration. Fromm derives a number of his ideas from Meister Eckhart's teachings to which he often turned for inspiration. In *The Art of Loving* he includes the following quotation from the 13th/14th century Dominican mystic and theologian:

> If you love yourself, you love everybody else as you do yourself. As long as you love another person less than you love yourself, you will not really succeed in loving yourself, but if you love all alike, including yourself, you will love them as one person and that person is both God and man. Thus he is a great and righteous person who, loving himself, loves all others equally.[51]

The final type of love which Fromm mentions in *The Art of Loving* is love of God. Fromm sees similarities between our relationship with God and other relationships in that they all strive towards union. Loving God, like other types of loving, is an answer to the need to address existential anxiety and separateness. However, since the present chapter focuses specifically on interpersonal relationships we will not examine Fromm's views on religion here. The reader is referred to Chapters 5 and 7 for a discussion of Fromm's historical analysis of how different religions have evolved as socially situated answers to our existential needs.

Unproductive ways of escaping from existential anxieties

In *The Art of Loving* Fromm highlights some of the more unsuccessful and often transitory ways in which people have tried to avoid the anxiety which a sense of separateness evokes. This serves as his basis for exposing difficulties in individuals, relationships and also particularly their social context.

Trance-like *orgiastic states* are one such escape mechanism. Examples include alcoholism and drug addiction. Fromm suggests that once the relief from separateness which can result from alcohol and drug consumption wears off, the individual is left with guilt and a heightened sense of alone-ness. This will drive him to further and increased drug use – paradoxically reducing any opportunities for more effective relating which might help to deal with anxiety in a less destructive way. A further example of such trance-like states is sexual orgasm, when not accompanied by loving care and respect: according to Fromm, it leads to temporary relief from anxiety but will not provide more intensive and productive relating: 'the sexual act without love never bridges the gap between two human beings, except momentarily'.[52] In *To Have or To Be?*, he claims that the pursuit of sexual pleasure in the sense of momentary 'peak experience' only leads to disap-pointment in its brevity. He contrasts this with the more long lasting expe-rience of joy which can be found in good relationships anchored in the loving orientation of the 'being' mode.[53]

A further unsuccessful, albeit calmer and more permanent, way of dealing with aloneness is achieved through *group conformity* when we follow routines in work and pleasure pursuits and strive for 'sameness'. In simply 'switching off' our fears and submitting to the banalities of everyday life we stave off anxiety but head for a poor trade-off. The price paid for this sense of security is loss of individuality and aliveness, the very qualities which Fromm sees as essential for the development of mature love.

The third unhelpful way in which we commonly attempt to resolve exist-ential anxiety looks more promising at first glance. It is perhaps initially surprising to see *creative activity* in his list of unsuccessful solutions. Fromm uses this term to describe the sense of unity which artists or workers achieve when immersed in creating new products. Such experiences are perhaps rare in the modern day 'thin air'[54] industry of routine occupations in which many of us deal with phone calls and emails and rarely get the chance to be absorbed in creating and admiring the completion of a finished product. However, even in the creative mode, Fromm still sees this type of union between worker and object as not entirely fulfilling our existential need because it is not interpersonal and thus does not address our quest for relatedness: 'The full answer lies in the achievement of interpersonal union, of fusion with another person, in *love*.'[55]

The social context of love

The unsuccessful attempts at resolving existential isolation feature strongly in Fromm's analysis of love in his contemporary society. He suggests that modern society has dealt with love erroneously. Too often we focus on being loved rather than on loving. We have become too narcissistic and self-centred in our approach to relationships. Also, a society focused on marketing and exchange of goods has treated love like an economic transaction ('what's in it for me?') rather than a capacity to move us to further growth and development. He suggests that even our current emphasis on 'fairness' misses the point. In his view there is a big difference between love and fairness. While love implies union and concern for others, 'fairness' involves a more distant and dispassionate weighing up of exchange, and one in which we may be particularly preoccupied with our own end of the bargain. The complaint 'it's not fair' is often motivated by our feeling that *we* are not getting enough.

In his analysis of love in its context of post-war Western society, Fromm does not hold back on criticism. With the assumption that culture has a large part to play in shaping our relating in society, including interpersonal relationships, he asserts that genuine brotherly, motherly and erotic love have been replaced by *pseudo-love* – and he comments on the *disintegration of love*. He claims that the values underlying capitalist societies and the fundamental principles of love are incompatible. Capitalist values of commodity exchange produce an emphasis on property and gain, and lead to alienated relationships in environments of routinized emptiness. This produces a 'social character' who is focused on presenting his own marketability and exchange value with the hope of his partner being a fair exchange or bargain. What results in most cases is a

> well oiled relationship between two persons who remain strangers all their lives, who never arrive at a 'central relationship', but who treat each other with courtesy and who attempt to make each other feel better.[56]

He describes such relationships, born of profit motive and routine, as 'egoism *à deux* ... which ... is mistaken for love and intimacy'.[57]

Fromm criticizes the hugely influential narrative of *romantic love* in our society, pervasive in books, songs and films. It encourages us to emphasize and anticipate a passive 'falling' in love and makes us approach relationships with inflated and unrealistic expectations. Such bonds are doomed to fail in many cases. He cites what he calls *idolatrous love* as an example of 'pseudo-love'. We often see this represented in romantic fiction where an intense 'love' relationship is based on one person seeing the other as the personification of all that is good and virtuous. These narratives imply that the 'worshipper' has lost a sense of self and of who she is as an individual, while the person idolized with this intensity has no chance of living up to such impossibly high expectations. Fromm claims that disillusionment and disappointment are pre-programmed in such relationships.

He has a similarly negative view of situations in which each partner becomes a spectator of other relationships in books, magazines and films. This alienates a couple from the here-and-now aspects of real love – love is experienced vicariously. In contrast, he regards love as an activity: we 'stand' rather than 'fall' in love[58] – or perhaps we can take this metaphor even further to capture its developmental aspects and suggest that we 'walk' or 'move' in love.

His criticism is also directed at common sense myths around relationships – for example the idea that love implies the *absence of conflict*. Conflicts which serve to clarify where each partner is coming from can help a relationship to develop and grow. Other researchers now also point to the role of some degree of conflict as helpful in establishing joint construction of a partnership, confirming some of Fromm's assertions.[59] Similar to some of Carl Rogers' ideas on the importance of good communication in relationships he claims that 'love is possible only if two persons communicate with each other from the centre of their existence'.[60]

Fromm regards extreme views concerning the *duration and ending of relationships* as fallacies: 'the idea of a relationship which can be easily dissolved if one is not successful with it is as erroneous as the idea that under no circumstances must the relationship be dissolved'.[61] In other words, some hard work on relationships will be useful, but there is no benefit in upholding an irretrievably empty one either. Again, we should perhaps not be surprised by his conclusions in view of his own life story: he experienced the growing distance in his marriage with Frieda Reichmann, while in his subsequent two marriages commitment lasted until the end.

A further negative aspect which he perceives in his society is its *preoccupation with sexuality*. He suggests that this is often the result of an empty searching for temporary relief from aloneness or seen as a technical issue: teamwork to achieve mutual satisfaction. As Fromm puts it 'Love is not the result of adequate sexual satisfaction, but sexual happiness …is the result of love.'[62] Thus it would seem more important for couples to work on their personal development and relating rather than their sexual technique. Ideally, this would take place within a society which values these qualities and does not emphasize personal gain and profit quite as strongly.

Fromm sees sex as 'an expression of life'[63] and felt that the more open attitudes of his contemporary society were preferable to the repression and double standards of previous times. However, he still criticizes what he sees as his society's preoccupation with 'instant sex' lacking in '*human* intimacy'.[64] Some of these ideas must have been seen as challenging in the context of the call for sexual liberation in the 'swinging sixties'. Yet their popularity (*The Art of Loving* became a bestseller) at that very time seems to lend support to Fromm's view that many of us were (and are) indeed searching for a deeper sense of personal meaning and relating.

Evaluating Fromm's views on love

An exploration of Fromm's ideas on relationships prompts similar critical concerns to those voiced in Chapter 2. Fromm's thoughts appear to be based on a collection of personal experiences, professional observations and a selection of pertinent ideas from philosophy, religion and literature. This will not satisfy those who demand more concrete statistical or experimental evidence in support of any claims.

However, Fromm's emphasis on the important role which love and relationships play in our lives and the effect they have on our well-being have certainly been confirmed in subsequent research. For example, positive relationships and the social support they provide have an important buffering effect on us in times of adversity[65] and play a significant part in our experience of happiness.[66]

Further criticisms levelled at Fromm's ideas concern the lack of emphasis on biological factors, his concept of love and his analysis of relating in a social context.

Fromm underestimates the *biological basis of our sexual behaviour and experience*. He encounters challenges from two camps in this area.

One of them comes from traditional Freudian psychoanalysts. As we have seen, Fromm shifts his version of psychoanalysis towards consideration of existential issues rather than libidinal pressures. For many traditionalists this was a step too far in that it abandoned key tenets of Freud's theory. Also, as Burston proposes, in turning away from Freudian libido theory Fromm could be accused of neglecting the powerful role of sexual drives and their part in motivating our behaviour.[67]

Evolutionary psychologists[68] would join ranks with such critics and argue that Fromm does not emphasize the biological functionality of our behaviour sufficiently. As we have seen earlier, Fromm does suggest that there are male/female differences, with men more anxious about their ability to 'perform' and women more concerned about being attractive. He links these patterns to behaviour and anxieties during sexual intercourse but stresses that social expectations of typically masculine or typically feminine behaviour play a very important part.

Evolutionary accounts of such differences would seem to be more convincing. They suggest that the tendencies which Fromm describes are to some extent correct. However, their origins are more likely to lie in behaviour patterns which have given us a reproductive advantage in our evolutionary past and have thus perpetuated the genes to which they are linked. Because women have a much higher investment in the results of sexual union – pregnancy and child care – evolutionary pressures have predisposed them towards selecting males with material resources who are high in status and are more likely to take care of them and their young children. Women would therefore be more careful in their selection of a partner and value *relationships* rather than brief sexual encounters. Men, on the other hand, are capable of inseminating many partners, and in order to maximize their reproductive success would tend to seek multiple, young, attractive partners. Buss[69] derives some support for his claims from cross-cultural observations and attitude questionnaire studies. For example, in a number of different countries more men were found to put physical attractiveness at the top of their list when asked what they look for in a partner. Conversely, women appeared to prefer economic security as a key attribute in their ideal man. However, such data are not entirely clear-cut either in that it is difficult to separate biological and social factors. Social and biological pressures combine to provide a complex picture in which it is difficult to estimate the relative importance of each set of factors. Neither biologists nor sociologists on their own are able to account fully for the vast array of different ways in which individuals live out their sexuality or choose not to express it.

Furthermore, such findings do not only show some differences between genders. The amount of commonality and overlaps is also striking. This provides fuel for Fromm's important argument that similarities between the sexes are larger than any differences and that 'men and women are first and foremost human beings sharing the same potential, the same wants and the same fears'.[70]

While we may argue that such an observation is simply common sense, this is an important message worth re-iterating in our times. A pre-occupation with gender differences certainly seems to pervade the current popular psychology literature, with the danger of interpersonal relationship issues and difficulties being explained away by reference to biology – whether evolution or brain patterns. When done in a superficial manner this runs the risk of entrenching expectations and limiting what each individual might be capable of. Perhaps, taking Fromm's sentiments forward, it is time to remind ourselves that the point is not so much whether men might be from Mars or women from Venus but that they are both from Earth.

Could Fromm be regarded as 'sexist' in following Bachofen's idea that paternal principles include reason in contradistinction to the maternal? Such assertions could be seen to resemble uncomfortably the sexist assumption of 'reason' as a male prerogative which in the past has served to justify keeping women out of universities and away from positions of power. However, Fromm claims that both polarities are reflected in us all. Furthermore he argues that maternal *and* paternal principles have positive and negative points. He highlights the importance of a balance of both modes to avoid the potential excesses of each. As Wilde[71] argues, in this sense, Fromm's views actually anticipate some feminist arguments which bring to light the destructive potential of oppression and exploitation; the dark side of what Fromm calls the paternal principle. Urgently needed social change in which concern for equality, care and compassion become guiding principles is more likely to come from maternal orientations.

We also need to examine Fromm's *concept of love*.[72] Is it really possible to capture all the many nuances of this experience under one term and see their ideal under the heading of one orientation; 'productive love'? Are there not too many differences between, for example, the experience of lovers, friends, the love from parent to child or love of oneself? We could argue that in Fromm's treatment of this topic, the word love becomes a straightjacket into which his humanistic values are squeezed even when there are apparent contradictions.

Fromm's explicit dichotomy of mature versus symbiotic love could be criticized for presenting a somewhat stark categorisation of human interaction, ignoring some of the shades of grey which colour our daily relating. Deciding at what point a relationship is to be characterized as symbiotic rather than mature could be rather arbitrary in that it involves assessments of the rather elusive notion of 'integrity' of each partner – clearly not an easy task.

Another point for discussion is Fromm's claim that in loving, including in erotic relationships, we love in the other person 'all of mankind, all that is alive'.[73] Schaar rightly comments on the difficulty with this assertion and presents a different view. He suggests the lover's smile does not reflect universal love for and solidarity with others as Fromm would have it, but it is a sign that – in his preoccupation with his beloved – 'he has funda-mentally overlooked them.... His smile is really a projection onto others of his own well-being, not a genuine concern for theirs.'[74] However, both sets of claims are difficult to assess and we are left with conjecture from both sides.

A further criticism of Fromm's view of love links to his suggestion that will, judgement and discipline underlie relationships. As we have seen above, he is rather negative about romantic notions of the 'magic' of falling in love. However, more recent evaluations of Fromm's ideas from experts in couples therapy have questioned this. Jellouschek[75] highlights the positive aspects of this experience and the powerful memories which these intense emotions engender. He points out that encouraging couples to reminisce on the time when they first fell in love can help a relationship regain lost magic and strengthen commitment to make a fresh start possible. He adds that in his view the intuitive quality of 'falling in love' is important and that Fromm perhaps makes love sound too much like hard work.

His strong condemnation of *relating in a social context* also seems rather negative. Such suggestions appear to reflect more than anything Fromm's own dislike of small talk and social chat, neglecting the possibility of initially 'trivial' conversations leading onto further deeper relating. While some of his dichotomous suggestions about qualities and orient-ations in our thoughts and actions encourage reflection and aware-ness, when refer-ring to people engaged in small talk as 'zombies... whose soul is dead' this comes across as prejudicial and dismissive of any-one not on his wavelength. His assertion that 'There are many people ...

who have never seen a loving person, or a person with integrity, or courage, or concentration'[76] – is a bold claim whose evidence base is unclear.

This also begs the question of whether his generally negative assessment of love in his *society* is justified. What should we make of Fromm's claims regarding the incompatibility of the principles of capitalism and love? Is productive relating really not possible in a society whose values of self interest appear to fly in the face of solidarity and love, caring and compassion? He claims that within the capitalist profit motive of Western society, people capable and committed to love will remain a small minority. Only more profound changes in our social system will allow us to express genuine love on a wider scale. He does concede, however, that given the complexities of modern society, 'a good deal of non-conformity and of personal latitude'[77] is possible. While it may be impossible to derive clear conclusions from such assertions, this emphasis on the societal context in which relationships are played out seems to be an essential ingredient in a more wide-ranging analysis of love.

Fromm also makes some rather startling suggestions such as 'not to be bored or boring is one of the main conditions for loving'.[78] This is perhaps not always realizable in our everyday living and might be more achievable in circumstances close to Fromm's own life-style which allowed for many stimulating events and activities. However, these criticisms should not deny the utility of his ideas as guidelines to aspire to and be inspired by. While many of us may not follow daily routines similar to Fromm's, it would seem a pity to lose sight of some of the transformational aspects of his ideas.

More generally, when looking at Fromm's ideas on love and his recommendations for relationships, it is easy to see how they can be related to his own life circumstances. For example, his choice of the term 'mature' love is interesting: when he wrote *The Art of Loving* he was middle aged, happily married, comfortably off and childless. It seems highly likely that his marriage with Annis Freeman gave him a sense of integrity and contentment – 'mature love' (*The Art of Loving* was published in 1956, three years after he and Annis were married). Annis, it seems, was certainly a mature and committed companion, who took a deep interest in Fromm's well-being and work. In contrast, previous relationships, especially his marriage to Frieda Reichmann, may have resembled a more symbiotic union, perhaps based on unresolved issues arising from his relationship with his mother, though, as pointed out in Chapter 1, this may be just one assessment of the situation, obvious because of the age gap between them.

What makes Fromm's ideas unique is that he does not look at human relating at only one level. To foster positive relationships we need to keep an eye on both individual development *and* on social conditions. Fromm's optimism is reflected in the last pages of *The Art of Loving*. 'To have faith in the possibility of love as a social and not only exceptional-individual phenomenon, is a rational faith based on the insight into the very nature of man.'[79] Whether or not we agree with his assessment of rationality and insight, Fromm has to be given credit for providing a thoughtful analysis of personal relationships which does not only examine them at one level but also provides tools for personal reflection and social analysis.

4 The Art of Psychotherapy

Fromm's psychoanalytic experience was extensive. He came into contact with psychoanalysis through Frieda Reichmann, his first wife, and he also trained in Munich, Frankfurt and Berlin where he himself worked as an analyst. After his move to the USA he started practising again in New York in 1934 and remained active in psychoanalysis and training of analysts during his time in Mexico. This chapter will explore some of Fromm's ideas about the therapeutic process and will focus in particular on the qualities to be developed in the patient and in the analyst, and on the nature of the relationship between them.

It is worth noting the language Fromm used in describing his ideas on the therapeutic process. Psychoanalysis was originally developed from a medical model reflecting Freud's training as a neurologist, evident in words like 'doctor', 'patient', 'symptom' and 'cure'. Fromm built his own approach on this and uses the analogy of x-ray to describe the therapist's finely tuned understanding of her patients' concerns. However, he also challenges what he saw as some of the more entrenched aspects of psychoanalysis and moves it away from a medical discourse. Working from a humanistic starting point, he regards the patient as an active participant in the process and makes some recommendations which go much beyond traditionally defined psychoanalysis towards more fluid ideas on personal development in a social context.

A Frommian 'technique'?

Fromm never wrote a book about his own approach to therapy, and there have been speculations as to why he didn't, given his generally productive writing in a number of diverse areas. Some suggest that he was not keen to pass on any specific points about 'technique'. For example, Lesser[1] claims that in the contact she had with Fromm in supervision he never gave any indication of wanting to capture a Frommian technique.

Chrzanowski[2] suggests another reason why Fromm did not write a book about his therapeutic technique:

> he did not want to start a Frommian school. He rejected blind allegiance to a leader which would negate his particular emphasis on the individual experience of a particular and unique psychoanalyst and patient dyad.

This certainly seems plausible given Fromm's suspicions of any dogma. His focus on the uniqueness of each encounter may also have gone against setting in stone his therapeutic methods.

However, Fromm did specify some essential components of his therapeutic approach. In the summer of 1974, Fromm and Bernard Landis, a psychoanalyst from New York, gave a seminar of several weeks' duration for American psychology students in Locarno, Switzerland. Excerpts from this were to form part of a future book on psychoanalytic therapy.[3] A text entitled *'Psychoanalytic "Technique" or The Art of Listening'*, which Fromm wrote shortly before his death, was intended to form the introduction. In this he emphasizes the *'rules and norms'*[4] that must be followed for an understanding of minds, and particularly their unconscious components.

As he did for loving in personal relationships, Fromm refers to psychoanalysis as an *art* in that its potential for creativeness and development depends on the commitment of both analyst and patient to be self-reflective and willing to learn. Funk sums up Fromm's approach as follows:

> His therapeutic method is characterized not by verbose theories and abstractions, nor by differential diagnostic 'rapes' of the 'patient material', but rather by his capacity for individual and independent perception of the basic problems of man. Fromm's humanistic view permeates his ideas about patients and how to deal with them. ... A profound solidarity is discernible between the analyzer and the analyzed. It assumes that the analyst has learned how to deal with him-or herself and is still ready to learn rather than to hide behind a 'psychoanalytic technique'.[5]

The essence of psychoanalysis: to know oneself

As we have seen in the previous chapters, Fromm regards our ability to become aware of the obstacles which hinder the development of our human potential as crucial. This is, of course, particularly important for people who are seeking treatment for neurotic symptoms such as anxiety or obsessional thoughts. Fromm saw Freudian psychoanalysis as an important way forward. Awareness and understanding of unconscious conflicts and previously unrecognized associations between events (which are revealed, for example, in our dreams) allow us to change and move forward.

Fromm agrees with the main aims of Freud's approach. However, Fromm's views on the details of the therapeutic process which can bring about such understanding vary from Freud's in some important aspects, as we will see below. One of the main differences between them stems perhaps from their starting points. Freud developed his psychoanalytic approach from a medical background. Fromm, on the other hand, was a sociologist whose emphasis on social conditions is apparent even in his approach to therapy. His focus on the interpersonal qualities of the analytic relationship also differs from Freud's approach in which the analyst is a more detached observer.

The key qualities of Fromm's view of love outlined in Chapter 3 not only apply to personal relating; they describe an orientation to oneself and others in all aspects of life. It is thus not surprising to find that Fromm's commitment to personal growth, empathy and love is also apparent in what we know about his approach to the therapeutic relationship. As his colleague Spiegel suggests: 'For Fromm the fulfillment of one's being psychoanalyzed is epitomized in the development of self-understanding, and in the capacity to relate to others with love.'[6]

Fromm describes his own approach to therapy as follows:

What do I do? I listen to the patient and then I say to him: Look, what you are doing here is the following. You tell me whatever comes to your mind. That will not always be easy. ... So I listen to you. And while I am listening I have responses which are the responses of a trained instrument. ... So what you tell me makes me hear certain

things and I tell you what I hear, which is quite different from what
you are telling me or intended to tell me. And then you tell
me how you respond to my response. And in this way we
communicate.[7]

According to Fromm, these 'responses of a trained instrument' have to be
fine-tuned through ongoing self-reflection and self-analysis.

Fromm's answer to the question as to the aims of psychoanalysis
is clear: 'that's a very simple question and I think there's a very
simple answer. To know oneself.'[8] In his description of the psychoanalytic process, this applies to the analyst as much as to the
patient. It is only through having a deep understanding of ourselves
that we are able to change, develop and grow and to promote this in
others.

Thus the process of analysis is also seen as a unique learning experience
for the analyst herself, crucially dependent on a self-reflective stance. This
is illustrated in an episode described by Akeret who was supervised by
Fromm:

So, Doctor, he said, what have you learned about yourself from
your patient?
I thought I had misheard him.
About him? I fumbled.
No, about *yourself*, Akeret. What you learn about him follows
from what you learn about yourself.[9]

This, of course, links closely to the psychoanalytic requirement for analysts to be themselves analysed in training, but Fromm also particularly
emphasizes the importance of maintaining self-reflective analysis beyond
the training stages.

Both for his own psychoanalytic practice and for supervision
of analysts, Fromm appears to have taken an individualistic approach
based on self-analysis and intuition. He transmitted this in his own style
characterized by immediacy, vitality and intensity: Gojman de Millán, a
Mexican psychoanalyst, suggests that

Fromm's approach to psychoanalytic practice and training
was not aimed at an intellectual transmission of external
knowledge, but rather at the awakening within the analyst

of a meaningful, honest, and profound interest in the
patient.[10]

Another supervision episode illustrates this. Akeret reports the following
exchange between him and Fromm regarding assessment of a patient:

> That's just my feeling, of course.
> *Only* your feeling, Dr. Akeret? He laughed. Tell me, what else do we
> have to go on in our work – signs from God?[11]

Similarly, Chrzanowski, also supervised by Fromm, describes Fromm's
encouragement to move on from preconceived and rigid Freudian ideas.
'He wanted to enable me to get in touch with my own creative visions
about a patient.'[12] This implies that the analyst has to have a keen sense
of his own hunger for development and curiosity in order to spark off
change and learning in the patient.

Fromm suggests that it is essential for the analyst to develop personal
qualities of compassion and understanding, and that self-reflection and a
general interest in the interweaving influences of the personal and the
social provide a key to this. He surmises that deep understanding of these
issues as well as of the unconscious is often captured in more moving and
interesting ways in literature rather than in textbooks:

> social analysis and personal analysis cannot really be separated ...
> Perhaps it is much more useful to the understanding of
> psychoanalysis to read Balzac than it is to read psychological
> literature. ... If one is really interested in man and his unconscious,
> don't read the textbooks, read Balzac, read Dostoyevsky, read Kafka.
> There you learn something about man, much more than in
> psychoanalytic literature (including my own books).[13]

Fromm's 'Humanistic psychoanalysis'

The focus on knowing oneself also forms the humanistic premise from
which Fromm worked: 'There is nothing in the patient which I do not have
in me.'[14] In this he distances himself from approaches which assume more
definite delineation between the patient as 'the sufferer' and the analyst
as 'the expert'. Fromm's humanistic starting point of removing some of
the distance between analyst and patient is expressed vividly in his claim

that 'We are all crazy, we are all neurotic, we are all children, and we only differ in the degree to which this is the case.'[15] He suggests that analysts cannot distance themselves from patients in setting themselves apart as 'normal' while their patients are seen as belonging to a different category in their 'irrationality'.

According to Fromm, the special relationship between analyst and patient, in which personal growth and insight are seen as so crucial is essential to successful psychoanalysis. In this, the American psycho-analyst Harry Stack Sullivan and his view of psychiatry as 'the science of human relationships'[16] was an important influence. The nature and intensity of therapeutic relating is best characterized by the term *productive relatedness* which, according to Landis, Fromm describes as follows:

> in the act of being fully engaged with the patient, in being fully
> open and responsive to him, in being soaked with him, as it were,
> in this center-to-center relatedness, lies one of the essential conditions
> for psychoanalytic understanding and cure. The analyst must become
> the patient yet he must be himself; he must forget that he is the
> doctor, yet he must remain aware of it. Only when he accepts this
> paradox can he give 'interpretations' which carry authority because
> they are rooted in his own experience.[17]

These are strong and inspirational words. Whether they can always be taken literally in the therapeutic process is perhaps open to question. On the other hand, an important point to take on board here is Fromm's emphasis on recognizing the commonality between us and others. The patient may experience distress or destructiveness to a greater extent. However this is not to say that the therapist cannot recognize aspects of such emotions or tendencies within herself. It is through this compassion and solidarity that she is able to develop productive relating with the patient.

Similar to his recommendations for personal relationships, Fromm high-lights the importance of *communication* and regards the analytic relationship as a special form of communicating which is based on mutual freedom and spontaneity. Through this process, Fromm argues, we can work on some specific factors which can lead to positive change through therapy:

1. The increase of freedom when a person can see his or her real conflicts.

2. The increase of psychic energy after freeing it from being bound in repression and resistance.

3. Freeing the innate strivings for health.[18]

This list bears close resemblance to the humanistic psychologist Carl Rogers' ideas on personal growth or self-enhancement. Despite such similarities Fromm distances himself from Rogers' humanistic 'person centred' therapy in which the counsellor mirrors or reflects back to the client, with the client basically in charge of the pace and duration of the therapeutic process. Fromm felt that the idea that patients should 'find themselves' only prolonged the process unnecessarily. In particular, he found Rogers' notion of 'client centred therapy' rather strange because, he argued 'every therapy has to be client centred'.[19] Nonetheless, we can see clear parallels between their approaches. Like Fromm, Rogers emphasizes the quality of relating in counselling and stresses the importance of unconditional positive regard, empathy and genuineness.[20] However, Fromm's maintaining of basic Freudian principles and his more active role in therapy form the demarcation line. He still saw himself as a 'psychoanalyst'. His preference for the term *humanistic psychoanalysis* reflects his allegiance to Freud's view of the unconscious yet his commitment to a more openly humanistic stance in therapy.

Face-to-face relating

Fromm acknowledges Freud's important contribution in focusing on the hitherto neglected emotional quality of the relationship between doctor and patient. Yet in some important respects he moves the therapeutic encounter into a different realm. Even though Fromm initially followed standard Freudian approaches in his own practice, he soon became critical of this. Instead of the analyst sitting next to a patient lying down as in traditional psychoanalytic encounters, Fromm liked to sit face-to-face with his patients. He felt that the couch had come to represent an empty ritual in which the patient was 'artificially infantilized'.[21] He points out that the original arrangement may have been due to Freud's discomfort at being 'stared at by another person for many hours a day'[22] rather than a requirement in terms of the efficacy of analysis.

In Fromm's experience the lack of eye contact and the instruction to interrupt the patient's talking as little as possible prompted tiredness and boredom in the analyst. He also notes that a number of his colleagues admitted to taking short naps during analysis; others fought this urge for fear that their snoring might give them away.

Around 1940 Fromm changed his technique, and patients were invited to sit in a chair facing him rather than lie on a couch.[23] Face-to-face relating with his patients allowed him to communicate with them on the same physical level, encouraging more direct emotional relating, too. He engaged his patients in intense conversation, putting back to them the meanings he picked up during the encounter. Face-to-face relating also gave him the opportunity to observe their facial expressions and establish and maintain eye contact, as well as allowing the patient to read his face:

> I don't try to hide anything in my face. This affords the patient another very important communication with reality. Additionally, there are some candid statements that should only be said face-to-face because the words are more real that way.[24]

The sense of intense connectedness which many people felt in his presence was surely an important tool in his therapeutic approach. For example, Funk[25] portrays Fromm's gaze as warm and yet direct, sometimes almost too intense, which made it feel as though he was able to look straight into one's essence. This gaze accompanied searching and direct questions which sparked off self-reflection. Similarly, Khoury[26] describes Fromm's clear, intense and open facial expressions which in turn invited his conversation partner to reciprocate this openness.

The extent to which those psychoanalysed by Fromm actually experienced therapy in this way is illustrated by Marianne Horney Eckhardt who was analysed by Fromm as part of her own training. Following the move from 'couch to chair' and from analysts listening impassively to meaningful exchanges, she describes that she '… felt addressed as a person and not as a patient'.[27]

Fromm's use of dream interpretation

In line with traditional Freudian approaches, Fromm saw dreams as an important manifestation of unconscious meanings.[28] In fact, in 1951 Fromm wrote a book entitled *The Forgotten Language. An Introduction to the Understanding of Dreams, Fairy Tales and Myths* based on his lectures at the William Alanson White Institute and Bennington College.[29] Examining the history of dream analysis in religious, historical and literary sources as well as exploring myths and rituals, he suggests that the 'language' of dreams is universal, symbolizing key experiences which arise from our shared human condition. Such claims may prompt the question of whether we can interpret dreams outside our socially and culturally constructed understanding. The emotion accompanying a dream that we are running late for a class only makes sense in a culture in which timekeeping is of the essence. Then again we could argue that, stripped of the details of such meanings, we really can trace deeper and more universal concerns in this: time keeping issues may link to more deep seated fears of rejection by those in positions of authority (though even this clearly carries cultural meanings, too).

In 1972 Fromm wrote an essay in which he takes a wide approach to the development of understanding dreams. He suggests that the dogmatic claim proposed by some traditional psychoanalytic groups to have the only answer to dream analysis should be challenged. Dreams do not necessarily need to be interpreted within the confines of psychoanalytic language: 'Usually I ask the person whom I analyze what he or she thinks about the dream ... fifty percent of all dreams you can understand without associations.'[30] This again shows Fromm's move away from the psychoanalytic ring fencing of psychodynamic insights and towards more fluid understanding of the role the 'expert' analyst should have in the encounter. His own interpretations did still play an important role: 'I tell the patient what I see and then analyze the patient's resistance to what I am saying.'[31]

Using historical evidence and case studies as examples, he argues that, traditionally, dreams have been seen as either heightened imagination or else, for example in Freudian approaches, as our instinctual – particularly sexual – drives seeping into our consciousness in encrypted form. Fromm argues that dreams can express both of these qualities. He suggests that in our dreams we can be more creative and feel that we possess faculties which we may not have during our waking hours: we may be able to sing, dance and fly – in contrast to our abilities when awake. Dreams allow us to express our creativity free of social expectations and convention. Fromm claims that 'sleep is the only situation where we are really free. ... In the dream we do not see the world as we have to see it when we want to manipulate it; rather, we see the poetic meaning it has for us.'[32] Taking a stance between Freud's claim of dreams reflecting unconscious conflict and Jung's idea that dreams represent higher wisdom, Fromm claims that *we are not only less reasonable and less decent in our dreams but...we are also more intelligent, wiser*

and capable of better judgment when we are asleep than when we are awake'.[33]
He suggests that the art of dream interpretation lies in knowing which
dreams represent our instinctual nature and which are expressions of our
creativity.

Fromm's style of therapeutic interventions

Fromm advocates a *direct approach* to therapy. The process of being
in a therapeutic relationship with him was certainly not seen as easy or
comfortable.

This is Lesser's description of Fromm's directness:

> There was no waiting for just the right moment, no hesitation about
> articulating his judgments, and no equivocation about just the right
> dosage of truth. With good-humored irony, he [Fromm] noted,
> 'There is nothing polite in anybody's unconscious, including the
> analyst's'.[34]

Fromm's aim was to induce patients to grow, move and change through
sometimes difficult insights, as Akeret notes:

> If tension, pain and deep feelings are not present, from where will
> come the desire for change? Analysis is as serious as the surgeon's
> incision or the Zen master's rap. The analyst must constantly ask
> himself, 'What is new that the person learned this hour or this week?'
> this allows the analyst to make an impact on the patient, which
> Fromm regarded as crucial.[35]

Fromm himself expresses this in a different, equally thought-provoking,
metaphor suggesting that the analyst's impact depends on

> whether he is able to do what a good mountain guide does, who
> doesn't carry his client up the mountain, but sometimes tells him:
> 'this is a better road,' and sometimes even uses his hands to give him
> a little push, but that is all he can do.[36]

He also moves the Freudian method of *free association* into a different realm.
Instead of ritualized formulae used at the beginning of the analytic session
'tell me what's on your mind' and then keeping interaction to a minimum,
he tried to develop new techniques. As a preliminary to a different type of
free association, he told his patients to concentrate and free their minds

from intrusive thoughts (for example, he instructed patients to imagine their minds as a blank screen and when he gave a signal the patient was asked to describe what he saw on the screen).[37] Some of these points show that Fromm was a very visual person, also illustrated in his emphasis on direct eye contact with people in therapy or supervision as outlined earlier.

Fromm highlights that his own individual style is full of *poetry and imagery*, which may have made it difficult to describe. In this he tries to distance himself from Freud: 'Freud had no real sense for symbolism, as he had no sense for art and poetry, he had a sense for that only which one could conceive intellectually.'[38] Although such an accusation is not justified,[39] Fromm uses it to contrast his own approach which he describes as follows: 'it is very important to see the patient as the hero of a drama and not to see him as a summation of complexes. And, actually, every human being is the hero of a drama.'[40] Landis[41] refers to Fromm's use of 'imaginative metaphor' in making explicit the 'rationalizations which have filled the patient's mind'.

Where Freud attempts to take adults back to the childhood origins of their unconscious conflicts, Fromm suggests that the patient must experience herself as an *adult and as a child*. This conflict between the patient's childhood memory and her adult experiences can be helpful in the therapeutic process. *'For me the essence of analytic cure lies in the very conflict engendered by the meeting of the irrational and the rational part of the personality.'*[42]

However, Fromm is realistic about what can be achieved in analysis. He accepts that change is not always possible and thus guards against unrealistic goals which only lead to disappointment and claims: 'It is important to show a healthy skepticism: "You say you want to change. It may be possible, but let's see".'[43] He also maintains a realistic sense of what role psychoanalysis plays in promoting positive change: Analysis can – but doesn't always – contribute to change, and people can change without analysis.[44]

Even if the therapy as such is not effective, Fromm suggests that time would still not have been wasted; in fact he makes rather bold claims about the benefits of analysis more generally: 'even in those cases in which a patient may not get well … the analytic hours, if they have been alive and significant, will have been the most important and best hours that he ever had in his life'.[45] In this sense he regards therapy as providing much more than a 'cure': he sees it as a way of liberating the self through awareness and the potential for change; an instrument in 'the art of living'.[46]

Regarding the *prognosis* and *duration of analysis*, Fromm felt that it was not necessary to prescribe how long the process needed to take: analysis should be as long as necessary depending on each case. In this, too, his ideas differ from Freud's.

> light forms of neurosis ... might be cured by methods much shorter than two years of analysis; that is to say, by having the courage of using analytic insight to approach the problem very directly, and possibly to do in twenty hours what one feels obliged to do as an analyst, in two hundred hours. There is no reason for false shame to use direct methods when they can be used.[47]

He does suggest, though, that this depends on the nature of the problem: not surprisingly he states that people with benign neuroses tend to have a better chance of a cure in comparison to those with more malignant neuroses.[48] Patients' general character orientations are also seen as an important factor in influencing his prognosis. Even if a patient suffers from a more severe illness, his chances of recovering are greatly increased if he approaches life from a more open, positive and biophilous stance. It is worth noting that although Fromm was supportive of severely disturbed patients and the analysts who worked with them, he often referred severe cases onto others who had fewer ongoing time commitments.[49]

To illustrate the sense of immediacy with which he used insights into the unconscious in therapy he describes the case of a woman whose life was marred by her obsession of having to return home as soon as she went out, fearing she might have left the gas on and have the house go up in flames. The process of analysis revealed that several years previously a surgeon who had operated on her to remove a cancerous tumour made a careless remark to her about the possibility of metastases spreading through her body like wildfire. Her fear of recurrent illness had shown itself in her obsession with fire in her house. Once the connection had been made, the woman – by then no longer afraid of the cancer returning – was free of her obsessive compulsion.[50]

Reevaluating the case of 'Little Hans'

A further point in which Fromm disagrees with Freud revolves around some of the conclusions which Freud drew in his analysis of his famous case of

'Little Hans', a boy who suffered from a horse phobia. Although Freud did not treat the boy directly, Hans's father corresponded with him regarding causes and treatment of the condition. The little boy's experiences at the time when the phobia emerged included seeing a heavy carthorse collapse, the birth of a little sister, a very close relationship with his mother, expressions of jealousy towards his father and attending a funeral.

Freud interpreted Hans's fear of being bitten by horses as an expression of his unresolved Oedipus conflict, the stage in boys' psychosexual development in which the child experiences an unconscious erotic desire for the mother and jealous aggression towards his father. This is accompanied by a fear that the punishing father would castrate him if he found out. The conflict is resolved by the boy trying to become like the father and taking on his values. In Hans's case Freud assumed that his aggression towards and fear of his father had been *displaced* onto an 'object' less close to home: horses.

In his very different interpretation of the case Fromm highlights the quality of relationships. He suggests that due to the close attachment between mothers and children in the early years, the emotional (positive or negative) impact of the maternal is stronger than the paternal influence. Hans's mother was explicitly negative to her son, telling him that she would leave him and threatening him with castration if he kept touching his penis. Fromm emphasizes that it is the intensity of relating rather than libidinous drives which set the tone for our development. Further, he surmises that fear of death may have been behind Hans's phobia since it coincided with his first experiences related to this.[51]

Fromm also proposes that in some sense Freud seems to collude with the establishment (i.e. parental authority) 'blaming' children for their 'incestuous fantasies' and viewing them as 'mini-criminals'.[52] Fromm assesses family relations in a very different light. Controversially, he states that '… the analyst should be the accuser of the parents. An analyst should have an objective view. But if he is the defender of the parents because that is the spirit of the establishment, then he will not do much good to the patient.'[53]

Redefining sanity

Fromm's strong and provocative statements about parental authority link to the radical humanistic movement towards therapy and psychiatry in his time: he agrees with R. D. Laing's assessment that family dynamics and unhealthy societies can be the cause of mental ill health.[54] According to Fromm, parental love can serve as a mask for parents' wish to exert power over their children in a negative and destructive way, with truly loving parents the exception.[55]

Furthermore, he also suggests that we have to take a wider view of what should be seen as 'normal'. He highlights the case of someone functioning 'normally' within the context of a particular society which can itself be seen as insane: 'How sick, really, is modern organization man: alienated, narcissistic, without relatedness, without real interests for life.'[56] Fromm's notion of the *pathology of normalcy*[57] describes the insanity which he perceives in consumerist society. The difficulty, then, would be to decide what an analyst could do for someone caught up in modern social structures. Despite his symptoms – defined as unhealthy according to Fromm's view of the person (see Chapter 2) – he appears to 'fit in' and is not deemed unwell.

In this sense Fromm's ideas on therapy inevitably lead to social critique, moving the issue of 'sanity' from the personal or interpersonal to the political realm.

Redefining transference

Similarly, his assessment of the notion of *transference* leads to social critique. In traditional psychoanalysis, the process of transference is a crucial component. The patient is assumed to transfer unconsciously some of her previous conflicted relating onto the analyst, such as a female patient relating to the analyst as if he were her authoritarian father while she becomes the dependent child. In the process of psychoanalysis this is then taken as the starting point for unravelling and hopefully resolving unconscious childhood conflicts.

Fromm takes on a very different interpretation of 'transference'. He suggests that transference processes as outlined above are anchored in our failure to deal with existential needs productively. Unable to cope with the fragility of our human existence, we develop a need to give over responsibility to the more powerful. The process of analysis would aim to help the patient recognize this and take charge of his own life.

Such processes can be observed in a societal context, too. Even as adults, unless we develop our potential for positive growth and relating, we may be unable to become free and rational in a society which militates against these qualities. The media, he argues, play a significant role in giving us a warped picture of life, and we remain insecure, powerless and frightened, only too willing to transfer responsibility onto figures of authority. Chapter 5 will take some of these points further.

Experiencing Fromm as analyst and teacher

With this strong emphasis on the qualities essential for the therapeutic process we may wonder to what extent Fromm himself displayed these. It certainly seems as though he had a profound impact on many people who describe the experience of energy and aliveness in analysis or supervision sessions with him. Funk suggests that

> Anyone who was in psychoanalysis with him sensed his relentlessness as a seeker of truth and as a critical companion as well as his extraordinary capacity for empathy, his closeness, and the immediacy of his relationship to others.[58]

On the other hand, there are also accounts of more volatile encounters as described by Chrzanowski:[59]

> Late night supervision at 11:30 P.M. was not exactly conventional. In addition there were times that he was late or did not show up at all. When my complaint about that reached his ears by way of Clara Thompson, he was quoted as saying that students should be glad to see him at all. Nothing was wrong with Fromm's sense of his own importance – perhaps one needs to have this sense to be as prolific and creative as he was.

Similarly, Lesser[60] observes that

> People have sometimes characterized Fromm as confrontational and judgmental in both his supervisory and analytic stance. This is perhaps understandable because unlike more cautious, traditional analysts he always focused directly on what he saw as the patient's core orientation and/or the supervisee's difficulty.

Then again other writers such as Tauber[61] claim that 'Fromm was a modest person; his forthrightness was not judgmental.'

These contradictory accounts suggest that Fromm was grappling on the one hand with the increasing pressure of being seen as a wise guru and on the other with his deep commitment to self-reflection and personal development. Enmeshed in a time in which traditional authority and dogma were widely challenged in the fields of psychiatry and counselling, he himself contributed to shaking up the system, sometimes in strong and uncompromising ways, at other times through reflection and his main message of commitment to love.

Burston's balanced analysis seems to capture some of the many different aspects of Fromm's impact:

> The record of his life bears witness to his courage, industry and ambition; his wit, wisdom, and compassion; and the sorrow, anger, and joy he experienced and embraced. Even when a certain arrogance, insecurity, and dogmatism occasionally come to light, there is very little evidence of callousness, complacency, evasiveness, or hypocrisy in Fromm's life and work.[62]

Evaluating Fromm's approach to therapy

As our discussion has shown, Fromm's views on the therapeutic relationship go beyond traditional psychoanalysis. They suggest a mix of approaches, partly psychoanalytic, partly humanistic, delivered in Fromm's idiosyncratic reflective and engaging style, and in any case not something which could be called a 'technique'.

Reading about Fromm's ideas on psychoanalysis and therapy, we can at times find ourselves drifting between Sigmund Freud and Carl Rogers, struggling to work out clear dividing lines. However, while Fromm distanced himself from orthodox psychoanalysis and Rogerian humanistic counselling, he clearly still saw himself as working mainly under the umbrella of psychoanalysis, preferring the label 'humanistic psychoanalysis'.

In borrowing and integrating aspects from different lines of therapy, Fromm opens himself to a range of criticisms from a number of camps. Humanistic psychologists would regard this emphasis on the unconscious as unduly deterministic. Orthodox Freudians, however, would question whether Fromm's extensions of psychoanalysis would still allow him to rank amongst them. And finally, those who regard any notions of the unconscious as unscientifically vague would reject Fromm's approach as being too close to Freud's in this respect.

Stevens[63] suggests that the value of psychoanalysis lies in offering us the tools for unravelling the subtleties of unconscious meanings. Such knowledge will not lead to hard and fast certainties but will involve provisional approximations to a deeper understanding of our psyches. As Fromm rightly points out, the analyst's continued openness to learning is crucial in this process. However, such a psychology of possibilities needs to formulate its conclusions cautiously, explicitly acknowledging its limitations. This is not the case for some of Fromm's strong assertions.

Whatever we make of the theoretical underpinnings of Fromm's approach, we must ask whether his interventions were successful. When requested to specify just how effective his method might be, Fromm was vague: 'I won't go into percentages now because in the first place that is a professional secret or trade secret, and in the second place one would have to talk a lot about it.'[64] Examining this statement in the context of 21st century publication of school league tables, surgeons' death rates in operations and calls for performance related pay, we realize just how far our questioning of experts has developed. In our critical stance towards professionals and expectations of transparency such statements would now be seen as unprofessionally evasive. While the testimonies included in this chapter show that on some people, at least, the effect of therapeutic interactions with Fromm was long lasting and life changing, it is impossible to evaluate his approach based on any more specific quantitative evidence.

The accounts presented here clearly suggest that the immediacy, intensity and aliveness of an encounter with Fromm had a dramatic effect on some of his patients and supervisees. Can we take this forward as a recommendation for professional relating? We may wonder to what extent anyone involved in counselling or therapy full time may be able to take on with every client the depth of emotional connection which Fromm recommends. 'to feel the experience of the other as if it were his own'[65] suggests an intensity which might make an analyst with a full case load unable to carry on working. Fromm, after all, was in a position of being able to pace his life between self-reflection, analysis and writing. This luxury is not open to full-time analysts or counsellors.

At the same time, though, Fromm emphasizes the mutually reinforcing properties of this aliveness of contact. Alertness, intuition and concentration in interaction lead not to fatigue but, on the contrary, mobilize further creativity and energy. Thus Frommian relating would actually help a therapist to maintain interest and focus. However, while this comes across as a refreshingly creative and intuitive approach it could equally be seen as dangerously unclear and unregulated, based on 'only feelings'. Fromm might reply that it is precisely the fine tuning of emotions and intuitions which make the analyst-patient relationship effective.

What is also special about his approach is the recognition of the mutuality of the relationship: 'the teacher is taught by his students, the actor is stimulated by his audience, the psychoanalyst is cured by his patient: provided they do not treat each other as objects, but are related to each other genuinely and productively'.[66] This statement suggests that the responsibility for a productive working relationship does not only lie with the teacher or the psychoanalyst but also with the student or the patient. Productive relating needs to be worked on in both parties. In this way, the *relationship* becomes the focus, not only the professional him- or herself. Improvement targets are not achieved through increased pressure on teachers or counsellors but through careful attention to the way in which the relationship can be developed from both 'centres'.

As we have seen above, Fromm made critical statements about the role of parents in causing unconscious conflicts and about the 'insanity' of social environments. He suggests that 'If you go through the life of most children, then indeed you will find that parental love is one of the greatest fictions that have ever been invented.'[67] This unnecessarily bleak view seems to ignore the mutual loving relationships which many parents and children share. It is, of course, true that families often have to weather emotional storms as they negotiate change and development. In some families dysfunctional relating leads to emotional and physical abuse. Equally, however, the very qualities which Fromm proclaims as the cornerstone of love hold together many families through often extraordinarily difficult circumstances.[68] It seems likely that his clinical experiences may have shown him a rather dark image of the family which omits another reality of shared love, respect, caring and joy.

Fromm's suggestion of the close links between societal conditions and family values also prompts further questions regarding what can be achieved in psychoanalysis. If individuals develop neuroses due to the negative environments of their parental home, and parents represent the negative values of an uncaring society, what exactly can a therapist do? On the other hand, it is also vital to acknowledge the link between individual and society in order to avoid redefining social problems as only individuals' responsibilities. This point will be taken further in Chapters 5 and 7.

The above exploration has outlined in some detail the importance of productive relating which Fromm put at the heart of his 'method' – and it is perhaps particularly apt to speak of the 'heart' of his approach. Appreciation of each person's uniqueness and a genuine curiosity in kindling in his patients and supervisees a spark of life and renewal come across as the hallmarks of his art.

It is perhaps appropriate to end a chapter on Fromm's ideas on therapy with an observation by Buechler:[69]

> I believe that Erich Fromm can inspire ... courage because he helps us have a strong sense of purpose about our work as analysts. Reading Fromm imbues me with the feeling I am fighting for *life* when I do my work. He encourages me to passionately promote fully living, to tend the life force in myself and others with my whole heart. This strong sense of purpose helps me brave the moral and emotional uncertainty of being a limited human being, and, nevertheless, profoundly influencing other lives.

5 What's Wrong with Society?

Erich Fromm was not only a writer and psychoanalyst; he was also an active campaigner for change and improvement in the way in which we organize our lives. His theoretical critical examination was coupled with practical suggestions for a better society. In an interview shortly before his death he is reported as saying: 'It is a strange thing, most people believe that in order to live a good life, one has not to practice.'[1] Fromm could certainly not be accused of taking such a detached approach. In addition to intense self-reflection, self-analysis and his therapeutic work, his concerns also included social issues. The list of Fromm's works from 1927 through to posthumous publications in 1994 reveals an impressive breadth of interest in historical and contemporary social concerns. As well as writing about psychoanalysis and society in general terms, he commented on political developments in post-war Germany, George Orwell's 1984, A. S. Neill's progressive Summerhill School, the Vietnam War and the Hippie movement. His involvement in different ways of improving society went beyond the messages which he published in books and articles; it included letter campaigns, symposia on humanistic socialism and activism at political party level. Unlike many other psychoanalysts of his time, he had studied sociology, and he maintained a lifelong interest in how social structures impact on individuals and vice versa.

This chapter will briefly reiterate the earlier exploration in Chapter 2 of what Fromm saw as the existential needs which we all have to face, but will relate them specifically to the social sphere. We will then examine his historical account of how particular social characters developed in relation to our needs. His investigation into the social character of German workers in the late 1920s will provide an example of how he saw social and individual processes as interlinked. This will be followed by an outline of his social critique of the society of his time and his suggestions for improvement.

The societal context of existential needs

Fromm offers a uniquely wide and encompassing view of what it is to be human, proposing a dynamic interrelationship between physical, psychological and social factors. His exploration of society firmly builds on his view of our essence. The key issue is that we lost unity with nature and were expelled from this 'paradise' of oneness because of our conscious awareness. Cut adrift from instinctual modes of behaviour and purpose, and yet still embodied creatures with all the frailties this implies, we are left with the question of how to find meaning in our existence of whose limits we are only too aware. While each of us has to come to terms with the tensions between our biological nature and our self-awareness, *societies* also develop their own characteristic ways of dealing with such issues. He suggests that society can be conducive to addressing existential needs productively or else stifle our development.

The first existential need is to be found in the tension between *relatedness and narcissism*.[2] Fromm holds up productive love as the key to resolving this constructively, accompanied by the qualities of '*care, responsibility, respect* and *knowledge*'[3] which underlie our experience of human solidarity.

The negative pole describes people failing to connect to others meaningfully and remaining locked in the illusion of their own reality. Only able to perceive the world in terms of their own needs and versions of events, they either submit to others and lose their own individuality or else deny others their integrity through domination. Linked to this is the defence mechanism of *authoritarianism*, described by Fromm as the 'tendency to give up the independence of one's own individual self and to fuse one's self with somebody or something outside oneself in order to acquire the strength which the individual self is lacking'.[4] Such strategies can be observed on a societal level too, for example when many people become attracted to a strong leader in fascist regimes. His analysis of the psychological processes underpinning the rise of Nazism in Germany focuses on the significance of authoritarian tendencies. As we will see later on in this chapter, Fromm's assessment of German workers' character orientations provides an example of these processes.

The *need for transcendence* is a further issue with which we have to deal. Two paths lead towards addressing this; a choice between 'creation and destruction, love and hate' which, he claims, 'are both answers to the same need for transcendence. ... However, the satisfaction of the need to create leads to happiness; destructiveness to suffering, most of all, for the destroyer himself.'[5] Destructiveness can be seen as an escape from a sense of powerlessness.

Fromm's third existential need is that of *rootedness*. Tensions come from a further polarity: *brotherliness versus incest* – his way of describing our ties to tradition. The loss of oneness with nature brought about by our capacity for awareness led to a sense of rootlessness. We can resolve this by progressing to a sense of mature connectedness and solidarity. The opposite pole is regression, what Fromm refers to as 'incest': *'by being bound to nature, to blood and soil, man is blocked from developing his individuality and his reason.* He remains a child and incapable of progress.'[6]

One particularly common form of remaining stuck in unhelpful familiar allegiances at the level of society is our 'love' of our country:

> Nationalism is our form of incest, is our idolatry, is our insanity.
> 'Patriotism' is its cult. ... by 'patriotism' I mean the attitude which
> puts the own nation above humanity, above the principles of truth
> and justice; not the loving interest in one's own nation, which is
> the concern with the nation's spiritual as much as its material
> welfare – never with its power over other nations.[7]

He also links to this a lack of 'objectivity' – the tendency for 'foreign' nations to be seen as utterly negative, in contrast to a picture of one's own country as the pillar of virtue. These sentiments may not be surprising from a man whose adolescence and adulthood were marred by the ravages of the nationalism which led to the First and Second World Wars. He experienced further examples of narcissistic nationalism when he wrote *The Sane Society* in the context of post-war and Cold War international tension and suspicion. In *The Anatomy of Human Destructiveness* he refers to such group narcissism as one of the main sources of international hostility.[8]

A *sense of identity* is another need which Fromm sees as fundamental to our existential well-being. He describes this as a way in which we can make sense of our experience of 'I'. He highlights that 'the need to feel a sense of identity stems from the very condition of human existence, and it is the source of the most intense strivings'.[9] This can be met productively by developing our *individuality* through mature and rational reflection. However, Fromm suggests that all too often a far less 'sane' response to this need is taken. We submerge our individuality in what he terms *herd con-*

formity to the extent that people will make all sorts of sacrifices to maintain this type of connectedness with their 'herd' (consisting of, for example, nation, class, and religion).

The final existential issue proposed in *The Sane Society* is the *need for a frame of orientation and devotion*.[10] We have to be able to make sense of our moral position in the world. Fromm claims that it is essential for us to have *some* frame of orientation even if this is illusory.[11] He emphasizes the functional similarity of most ideologies and religions: while their contents differ, they share the common factor of satisfying this need. When considering which systems should be seen as positive and which as negative, he sidesteps the issue. He claims that the world would be a better place whether we live according to the values of, for example, the Buddhist Eightfold Path *or* the Ten Commandments in the Bible. The main problem, as he sees it, is that people do not live according to the moral standards behind their beliefs but submit to ideologies which are at odds with the values of solidarity and love. *Common humanistic principles* are to be regarded as the ultimate yardstick for evaluating any system of thought: 'solidarity of all men and the loyalty to life and to humanity ... must always take precedence over the loyalty to any particular group'.[12]

Social character in a historical context

According to Fromm, historical analysis is necessary for an understanding of how the needs for *freedom* and *relatedness* are linked to character structures prevalent in modern societies. Of particular importance is the development of individualism (supported economically by capitalism and spiritually by Protestantism) from the late Middle Ages onwards.[13] According to Fromm, such an analysis can give us deeper insight into the development of fascism and modern democracy.[14]

He highlights that one of the key characteristics of medieval society was a deep connectedness between people, to the extent that individuals did not really have a concept of themselves as separate from society. On the one hand this meant that questions around the meaning of life were easily answered or often did not even arise. Meaning derived from social structures such as church and state – firmly rooted in a society which gave the individual little scope for choice. The price for this sense of being sure of and safe in one's place in the social and metaphysical order was subjugation to the rigidity of social structures.

Towards the end of the Middle Ages, Fromm claims, a new, more fluid, sense of individualism developed. *'The individual was left alone; everything depended on his own effort, not on the security of his traditional status.'*[15] These changes in terms of how people made sense of their lives were influenced by, and in turn encouraged the improvement of, technology: for example, mechanical clocks were developed and new attitudes to work arose.

During this era, Fromm suggests, we lost our sense of security and belonging. Old structures were no longer seen as immutable and a new sense of freedom began to pervade scientific and religious discussions. Traditional ecclesiastical structures became shaky with the development of Protestant ideas. Luther and Calvin put forward their notions of a much more individualistic relationship with God, challenging the corruption of the Catholic papacy of their time. While this brought with it hitherto unimaginable individual freedom, it was accompanied by growing insecurity and isolation.

Fromm describes the development of a character structure specific to the conditions of emerging Protestantism and capitalism thus:

> Protestantism was the answer to the human needs of the frightened, uprooted, and isolated individual who had to orient and to relate himself to a new world. ... Those very qualities which were rooted in this character structure – compulsion to work, passion for thrift, the readiness to make one's life a tool for the purposes of an extrapersonal power, asceticism, and a compulsive sense of duty – were character traits which became productive forces in capitalistic society and without which modern economic and social development are unthinkable ... [they] in ... turn become important factors in further economic development and influence the social process.[16]

One psychological response to these developments was an *authoritarian orientation*. This characterizes people who, fearing freedom, submit to higher authority and dominate those they see as beneath them. Fromm uses a psychoanalytic interpretation of Martin Luther's life to illustrate the way in which such orientations developed during this time. Luther is more often thought of as a rebel and challenger of the status quo in his defiance of Pope and established church.[17] However, in *Escape from Freedom*, first published in 1941, Fromm describes him as a fundamentally authoritarian character.[18] This orientation manifested itself in Luther's view of our relationship to God as one of self-denying surrender. Luther also advocated submission to worldly authorities in rather florid terms, and Fromm includes the following quotation from Luther's writings to substantiate his assessment: 'God would prefer to suffer the government to exist, no matter how evil, rather than allow the rabble to riot, no matter how justified they are in doing so. ... A prince should remain a prince, no matter how tyrannical he may be. He beheads necessarily only a few since he must have subjects in order to be a ruler.'[19]

Fifteen years after the publication of *Escape from Freedom*, fellow analyst Erik Erikson also offered a psychoanalytic perspective on Luther. He actually visited the Fromms in Mexico while working on this[20] (though it seems that Fromm and Erikson did not engage in extensive exchanges of ideas[21]). Erikson focused his analysis of Luther more specifically on identity development rather than social conflict. The different angles from which both writers approach the same character reflect their own interests as well as the dominant issues of the times in which they were developing their ideas. The backdrop to Fromm's views was Hitler's Nazi regime, in which he saw authoritarianism as a dominant feature. Erikson, on the other hand, wrote about Luther in a post-war era of increasing freedom and choice in which he regarded the search for identity as playing an important role.

Although Fromm is well known for his critique of capitalism, he does emphasize its importance for our development towards personal freedom. The ability of the individual to improve his social standing through work and accumulation of wealth offers new freedom: our social background was no longer the only factor affecting our achievements. Hard work could also lead to a better lifestyle. In this sense capitalism and Protestantism contributed to the development of an active, self directed and responsible individual. These points are important in that it is easy to overlook them in the light of Fromm's generally acid social critique.

The early years of capitalist societies offered the individual new possibilities for freedom but in terms of human relating, domination and exploitation severely limited the extent to which we could develop a humanistically orientated society. In industrial relations, for example, powerful factory owners clearly had the upper hand over workers whose rights were extremely limited. According to Fromm, progress towards humanism would build on the increases of personal freedom from previous eras in the context of a supportive society based on solidarity. However, he suggests that we have not progressed in this positive way. Instead of fostering freedom and loving relationships, we have allowed the lures and excesses of consumerism to become our masters.[22]

Before we turn to the key points of what Fromm thought was wrong with his contemporary society, we will examine how he applied his ideas to research into psychological and social developments in sections of German society on the eve of the rise of Nazism.

Social character analysis of German workers in the 1920s

Fromm builds his ideas on the interaction between individual and society on the following assumptions: societies are organized in different ways (for example around production and distribution methods). We can thus observe particular sets of conditions such as different styles of work, education and family systems. Individuals' psychological needs have to fit in with and also affect some of these arrangements. This then leads to a process of dynamic adaptation between social structures and individual psyche, with social changes giving rise to, for example, new needs and concerns. New ideas can 'suddenly' take hold because they key into psychological processes at the level of the individual. They in turn then become widespread and normative in society and will affect not only how individuals behave but also how society organizes itself. For example, social structures may create fear and envy in certain sections of the population. These emotions affect individuals' psyches and make them more susceptible to ideologies which promise to address these concerns.[23]

In his early work, in collaboration with several colleagues, Fromm used some of these ideas to conduct a questionnaire study into German workers' political and ideological orientations. This work was carried out under the auspices of the Frankfurt Institute for Social Research in the late 1920s, and interest in his concept of an authoritarian character structure continued there for well over ten years.[24] Fromm's research tries to apply some of the principles of psychoanalysis – the investigation of what is unconscious and behind the obvious – as a method to explore systematically some of the dynamics between individual and social conditions. It is also an attempt to bring together psychoanalytic principles and Marxist theory.

The questionnaire included items about workers' political orientations, personal tastes and general values on all sorts of issues, such as discipline of children and attitudes towards women's fashions. We can only marvel at the range and level of detail of the 271 questions asked, for example philosophical and political items: 'Do you believe that the individual is responsible for his own fate?', and 'How do you think a further world war can be prevented?' or general questions on lifestyle: 'What type of spread do you use on bread: Margarine – Butter – Lard – Jam ...?.'[25]

Not surprisingly, given the amount of time and willingness for reflection and disclosure, as well as the literacy skills required for such a detailed questionnaire, return rates were fairly low: 3300 were given out – passed on through various agencies like doctors' surgeries and libraries – and about a third were returned. As Fromm admits himself, there are limits as to the extent to which personal questions can be asked, and dangers that a questionnaire which is too detailed will be seen as an infringement of privacy.[26] Still, this must have produced a huge amount of data. With the frequent moves and upheavals in Fromm's own life in the 1930s, subsequent work on the questionnaires became rather fragmented.

Publication had been planned for 1936 but Fromm's increasing estrangement from the Institute for Social Research prevented this. It was only in the late 1970s that the German sociologist Wolfgang Bonss returned to the information still available and published the study in 1980.[27] He gives two reasons why he felt that it was important to make this material accessible. First, it provides an impressive historical account of some of the concerns and issues prominent in the lives of sections of the German population during the economically and politically turbulent Weimar Republic years of the 1920s. Fromm's work also deserves to be acknowledged as part of the history of research carried out under the auspices of the Institute for Social Research.

The following assumptions underlie Fromm's approach: he suggests that left wing parties of the time (relatively successful with the electorate before Hitler's ascent) promoted particular views of the world rather than just addressing political questions. Their ideologies included the principles of equality, freedom and peace, and solidarity with the oppressed. These values could thus be expected to be evident in the character structure of the people who voted them. Fromm saw the expression of these ideals as linked to a 'revolutionary' personality profile.[28] Its opposite would be the 'authoritarian' character orientation outlined earlier, going against the notions of freedom, tolerance and solidarity at the core of the 'revolutionary personality'.

Questionnaire responses were analysed to reveal unconscious expressions of these value systems. Fromm found discrepancies between manifest political identification and underlying character structures: for example, a number of workers predictably leaned towards the political left in openly political questions, but showed authoritarian orientations in less identifiably political items about, for example, discipline in families.

Fromm distinguishes between different response patterns.

For some people (about 15%), political leanings and ideological convictions appeared to match. They were fervent supporters of the principles of equality, tolerance and peace. Fromm suggests that they would have been the most likely group to resist Hitler's machinations, and many people with socialist convictions did indeed perish in concentration camps.[29]

In contrast, others (about 10%) appeared to show authoritarian character structures. They may initially have supported left wing parties not because of their ideals but because they were motivated by greed, envy and the hope that social change would give them a share of power and wealth. This group would have been more likely to become active supporters of the Nazi regime in that it personified their oppressive values and authoritarian leanings.

The majority (about 75%) were classed as not particularly fervent on either side but displayed a mix of orientations. Fromm and his colleagues suggested that this group would be open to Nazi propaganda (though with less conviction than the former group) which targeted their emotions and meshed with the aggressive/authoritarian aspects of their psychological make-up.

His conclusions contribute to an explanation of the seamless move towards Hitler's Nazi rule: despite the radical ideologies of the political left wing parties, the values which they represented may not have been part of the character structure of the people who voted for them.

However, the validity of these findings can be questioned. After all, response rates were low, and the sample may not have been particularly representative. We may also want to question whether we really can infer 'unconscious' value orientations from answers about attitudes and preferences. Fromm emphasizes that his own concern was with 'tendencies' rather than exact figures and correlations.[30] Nonetheless, we can ask whether it is possible to deduce stable character orientations from such questionnaire replies.

Whatever views we take of the validity of Fromm's concept or method, this study remains a fascinating mirror of its time. Anyone trying to gain a detailed account of the lifestyles and tastes of German workers in the late

1920s will find rich information in Fromm's data. Responses to questions about, for example, views on married women in paid employment, enjoyment of jazz music and household furnishings provide a snapshot picture of the lives of 'ordinary' people in a society marching towards fundamental change and conflict.

The problems of post-war society: alienated individuals in 'insane' societies

In terms of social critique Fromm's main area of interest was an analysis of his contemporary society in the USA and the ways in which this conflicted with what he regarded as the essential qualities of human nature. He outlines a critical analysis in a number of major publications such as *Escape from Freedom* (1941), followed by *Man for Himself* (1947) and *The Sane Society* (1955). This thread continues in *The Revolution of Hope* (1968), his most openly political book, written during the time when he supported Democrat Eugene McCarthy's presidential candidacy. It is also apparent in his final book *To Have or To Be?* (1976). Fromm's message in these books is clear: in a number of important ways modern society fails to meet our essential needs and does not provide an environment conducive to our optimal development.

Although Fromm does not deny the fact that modern society has also had many positive effects on us he generally tends to focus on its negatives. This is an interesting point to note in relation to the socio-economic context of his time. *The Sane Society* was written in the 1950s, a period of recovery from the effects of the Second World War and of high hopes in scientific, economic and technological progress. During this time, a 'golden age' of optimism, social critique must have seemed far from many American people's minds. With increasing tensions between the West and the Eastern bloc, Fromm's socialist ideas would have been viewed with intense suspicion. Funk reports that his political efforts did in fact attract a close eye from the FBI who kept a file on him of some 600 pages.[31] However, as Burston highlights, it is surprising that Fromm's outspoken opposition to Cold War and Vietnam War politics did not result in more direct persecution experienced by others who voiced similar criticisms.[32]

In what ways, then, does Fromm see his society as unable or unwilling to provide conditions conducive to the development of the healthy, productive person? He paints a bleak picture for society in the 20th century. 'In the 19th century the problem was that *God is dead*: in the 20th century the problem is that *man is dead*.'[33] He predicts that unless urgent action is taken, negative trends will continue within a system in which 'alienation and automatization leads to an ever-increasing insanity. Life has no meaning, there is no joy, no faith, no reality. Everybody is "happy" – except that he does not feel, does not reason, does not love.'[34] Fromm puts forward the notion of the *'pathology of normalcy*, particularly ... the pathology of contemporary Western society'.[35] Insanity need not be confined to disturbed individuals. *Societies* may develop dysfunctional structures and patterns of interaction which can become so dominant that the majority of people do not even realize that their human needs are not being met.

The dangers of consumerism

Fromm saw the majority of people in his society as alienated, drifting aimlessly in the bleak surroundings of empty consumerism:

> The passiveness of man in industrial society today is one of his most characteristic and pathological features. He takes in, he wants to be fed, but he does not move, initiate ... Man's passiveness is ... one symptom among a total syndrome, which one may call the 'syndrome of alienation'.[36]

Consumerism had become our unproductive way of dealing with insecurity and powerlessness, the hallmarks of 20th century developments. While society may have become wealthier, our sense of anxiety, boredom and aloneness has not been addressed: 'Everybody is coaxed into buying as much as he can, and before he has saved enough to pay for his purchases.'[37] Advertising encourages individuals to define themselves through the purchase of goods which may even harm their physical health – such as the tobacco and alcohol.

These processes require people who on the one hand feel 'free' but on the other are malleable enough to buy into this system of consumption. They conform to the dictat of the market forces while harbouring the illusion that they have done so of their own free will. He heaps the problems of modern society firmly on the door of capitalism. A society in which commodity exchange is everything does not do justice to human qualities: it commodifies human interactions and reduces them to economic exchanges.

A further specific negative aspect which Fromm sees as heightened by consumerist society is the principle of non-frustration. We expect every whim to be satisfied instantaneously – perhaps also evident in the high accumulation of personal debts, which is certainly a feature of 21st century Western capitalism. This differs from people's behaviour in previous eras: 'the classic representatives of capitalism enjoyed working – not spending'.[38]

Fromm acknowledges that an analysis of modern society could be approached from a number of angles depending on the 'particular interest of the investigator'.[39] Perhaps we should not be surprised by Fromm's choice of a focus on alienation. He himself must have found the post-war consumer boom in the USA entirely alien to some of the values of his European pre-war upbringing in which education and learning appear to have been favoured over consumption and acquisition. He claims that this alienation leads to a deep sense of unhappiness which is only fuelled by our futile attempts to buy ourselves out of our fundamental aloneness.

Conforming to irrational authority

The 'syndrome' of alienation seems to have been exacerbated during the post-war years in a climate of burgeoning information industries and technology. Although we are no longer tied as closely to the rigidity of traditional sources of authority such as church and state, our freedom may to some extent be illusory. *Authorities* have become anonymous, more fluid and less tangible, linked to an increasing climate of impersonal bureaucracy and routinized work situations.

Automaton conformity appears to be the main defence mechanism which modern societies have developed to cope with existential isolation. By becoming like the majority and following its patterns we develop a sense of security but pay the price of losing our individuality. This process of conformity is often insidious and difficult to trace because we simply accept what appears 'normal' and 'natural'.[40] Society's values militate against us developing productive orientations in tune with our human needs. The potential for individuality and freedom is there but we do not realize it.

The *political process* itself is also implicated in the alienation syndrome. Democracy is in danger of becoming nothing more than an exercise in manipulation:

> In an alienated society the mode in which people express their will is not very different from that of their choice in buying commodities. They are listening to the drums of propaganda and facts mean little in comparison with the suggestive noise which hammers at them.[41]

In this context Fromm also refers to a *democratic* orientation which describes people who respect their rights and those of others and who feel that everyone should be involved in decision making. Humanistic values underlie this orientation and it acknowledges *rational authority*. In contrast to imposed authority, this relationship is based on expertise as between, for example, a competent teacher and a willing pupil. As the pupil learns, the gap between them will close and the relationship will become one of equals.

Evidence for the syndrome of alienation

Sane societies need to be built on these humanistic foundations, or else we suffer from alienation. Fromm argues that the organization of modern societies alienates us to the extent that mental illness could in some cases be seen as a rational response to insane conditions.

For Fromm, the word 'sane' obviously conveyed an important message about how society should be organized. It features in the title of the book (*The Sane Society*) which explicitly deals with his ideas on how society fails to be essentially 'human'. SANE is also the name of the non-governmental organization in the US campaigning for nuclear disarmament in whose foundation he was involved. As Jack[42] highlights, this title is not an acronym but a word which Fromm found particularly apt as a name for a group campaigning against what he saw as the madness of the global arms race.

To back up his view that society, in its lack of consideration of the basic fundamentals of our existence, fails us and makes us ill, Fromm turns to data supporting his notion of malaise in society. He takes rates of suicide and homicide (both termed 'destructive acts'[43]) and the incidence of alcoholism as objective markers of alienation on a social scale. Acknowledging some of the difficulties in working with these rates (such as countries differing in their likelihood of recording suicide as a cause of death) he nonetheless claims that the more affluent countries (in 1946 terms) such as Denmark, Switzerland and the United States showed higher rates of these markers than did relatively poorer countries such as Norway and the Republic of Ireland. Based on his line of argumentation, Fromm concludes that 'the countries in Europe which are among the most democratic, peaceful and prosperous ones, and the United States, the most prosperous country in the world, show the most severe symptoms of mental disturbance'.[44]

Interestingly, both Norway and Ireland are now among the richest countries in Europe in terms of GDP per capita.[45] More recent measures of suicide do not include either the USA or Ireland as particularly high, though Norway has slightly higher rates, and the Swiss figures are still amongst the highest.[46] However, we also have to note that these statistics reflect different society's attitudes to the complex meanings of suicide: For example, in Switzerland it is legal for terminally ill patients to end their lives – an option which can be seen as an active choice rather than a sign of depression and alienation. We must question to what extent such crude measuring tools accurately reflect the precise nature of a particular society's psychological make-up. Some of Fromm's statements are prone to over-generalization. Nonetheless the key issue here is Fromm's claim that a seemingly wealthy society need not be a fulfilled one. This point is worth pursuing; both from his historical perspective and from our assessment of Western society from the vantage point of the 21st century (see Chapter 7).

How to put society right

While Fromm's social analysis can at times have a quality of fire and brimstone, there is a strong streak of optimism running through his work. Prophet-like, he points to a clear path either way: one which guides us towards salvation and one which appears to lead to negativity and destruction. These suggestions sound like a political manifesto, or perhaps even more so, a religious sermon, reflected in questions like: 'Will the majority be converted to sanity – or will it use the greatest discoveries of human reason for its own purposes of unreason and insanity?'[47] He sees our choice as a basic one between rationality – increasing humanism – and irrationality – a mechanized destructive society.

His suggestions for a sane society can be summarized in the following statements:

> a society in which no man is a means towards another's ends, but always and without exception an end in himself; hence, where nobody is used, nor uses himself, for purposes which are not those of the unfolding of his own human powers; where man is the center, and where all economic and political activities are subordinated to the aim of his growth. A sane society is one in which qualities like greed, exploitativeness, possessiveness, narcissism, have no chance to be used for greater material gain or for the enhancement of one's personal prestige. Where acting according to one's conscience is looked upon as a fundamental and necessary quality and where opportunism and lack of principles is deemed to be asocial; where the individual is concerned with social matters so that they become personal matters. … A sane society, furthermore, is one which permits man to operate within manageable and observable dimensions, and to be an active and responsible participant in the life of society, as well as the master of his own life. It is one which furthers human solidarity and not only permits, but stimulates, its members to relate themselves to each other lovingly; a sane society furthers the productive activity of everybody in his work, stimulates the unfolding of reason and enables man to give expression to his inner needs in collective art and rituals.[48]

These recommendations for *humanistic communitarian socialism* come across as a powerful wish list. Their realization, however, raises complex questions, some of which will be discussed below. One thing which Fromm is very clear about is that change can only come about by speedy, progressive reform and not revolution: 'I believe that the only force that can save us from self-destruction is reason … Violence and arms will not save us; sanity and reason may.'[49] Thus, education and information need to be at the centre of any reforms. Our starting point needs to be 'Planning which involves the system Man and which is based on norms which follow from the examination of the optimal functioning of the human being.'[50]

He proposes that changes have to be made in the economic, political and cultural organization of society. Not only does he give suggestions for all three areas, he also claims that they all have to change simultaneously: 'Changes restricted to *one* sphere are destructive of every change.'[51] This claim moves his ideal even further outwith the reach of potential realization.

The productive alternative to alienated work patterns

Work, to Fromm, plays a key role in ensuring that we remain connected to the social system in a productive way. It also provides psychological satisfaction in giving us a sense of purpose and meaning in a cooperative context. He highlights the benefits of various aspects of socialism, in particular the notion of workers' active involvement in workplace management. However, he questions the importance some Marxists put on economic factors *only*, ignoring the complexity of the human psyche, including moral aspects and human relationships. He points out that many followers of Marxist doctrine became caught up in 'sterile dogmatism'.[52] In contrast, Fromm emphasizes the benefits of looking at work and workers' relationships in line with communitarian socialists. They include, for example, followers of the traditions of Robert Owen[53] who promoted industrial relations in accordance with humanistic values, providing housing and education for his workers and encouraging active community involvement. Fromm formulates his ideal as follows: *'every working person would be an active and responsible participant, where work would be attractive and meaningful, where capital would not employ labor, but labor would employ capital'*.[54]

In the second half of the 20th century, he argues, this was not the case. Comparing previous working conditions of, for example, the artisan producing a quality product with industrial mass production, he regards alienation as a main feature of the modern production process. We are not directly in charge of what we produce any more. Instead, technology and production targets have developed a dynamic in which the individual is powerless and her contribution to the end product no longer carries any intrinsic meaning.

According to Fromm, we need to restore meaning in work and give back to the worker a sense of his own worth. His practical suggestions towards this end hinge around the notion of well-informed workers who are actively involved in every aspect of organizational structures and processes.

Can Fromm's ideas be realized? A number of doubts can be raised. First, people might simply be too lazy to approach work in such a conscientious fashion and might try to get away with the least possible effort. Fromm retorts that laziness itself is a sign of malfunctioning economic relations and that our natural and healthy state is one in which we enjoy productive activity and find boredom oppressive. Thus, he argues, produce the right socio-economic conditions and the right attitude to work will follow.

Second, if workers' choices and control over their work situations are seen as essential, would people really freely choose to opt for the more unpleasant jobs? Fromm dismisses this objection rather curtly and claims that this problem would solve itself through the diversity of people's inclinations: 'there is hardly any kind of work which would not attract certain types of personalities'.[55] This is a bold claim: labour shortages and subsequent efforts to attract economic migrants (based on financial rather than personal rewards) offers evidence against his ideas.

Some of Fromm's suggestions might well be applicable to those occupations which carry an intrinsic reward and where the worker is largely in control of her pace and product – for example an artist. Similarly, the creativeness of human relationships may provide such fulfilment for a teacher or a nurse. However, the reality is also that society needs people to carry out meaningless mind numbing tasks for its functioning. Workers' motivation in carrying out these jobs is almost purely financial. Nevertheless, Fromm's call for more humanistic working practices could at least help to improve conditions in those jobs.

Fromm also suggests that choice and freedom in the employment situation need to go further – and we can observe some progress towards this in the 21st century working practices of some countries. He proposes a guaranteed minimum subsistence allowance for every citizen which would be administered via the social security system and could be claimed for up to two years. Workers would then be able to take time off their work for personal reasons or in preparation for different employment if they needed the stimulation of new challenges. This would remove fear and anxiety in employees – for example not daring to speak up in case their jobs were in jeopardy – and would instead promote mutual respect between employee and employer and thus serve to promote creativity in the worker. Funding for such a scheme would come from saved costs which arise from the fallout of unhappy industrial relations causing, for example, stress related illnesses.[56] This would bring with it the attractive prospect that there would be no more dissatisfied workers in key roles hanging on to their job for economic reasons even though their enthusiasm and commitment are long gone. A new challenge could help them to move away from aspects of their work which they no longer find stimulating or suitable for their particular stage in life.

The productive alternative to insane consumption

While welfare systems provide safety nets of varying levels of tightness, Fromm's ideas go further in his advocating of 'Changing of the consumption pattern in the direction of consumption that contributes to activation and discourages "passivation".'[57] He challenges our obsession with material goods and suggests a redirecting of resources. He proposes that instead of manufacturing unnecessary private consumer goods, our efforts could be focused on, for example, community amenities, housing, public transport and cultural community initiatives, prompting a shift from private to public sector activity. He spells out his proposals more directly in an exploration of the *Psychological Aspects of the Guaranteed Income*,[58] published in 1966. He advocates for example, free access to medical care, education and cultural activities as well as free basic food and free housing. Such measures, he surmises, would have a profound impact on our psychological orientation. He observes that Western societies were about to enter into a state of abundance, which would leave their citizens free to invest their energies in more creative and related lifestyles. This would allow us to move away from a society in which people are in competition for scarce resources and are thus likely to develop greed and envy.

Fromm accedes that this is a challenging system for us to envisage since we are deeply anchored in the assumptions of competitiveness characteristic of previous eras. He predicts, however, that once we know that we can get access to basics such as bread and fruit at any time, greed would subside and a more general sense of solidarity could be developed.

In tandem with such developments, Fromm highlights the importance of changing our system from one of maximal consumption to one of *optimal consumption*. His evidence that such a system could work comes from our use of free public amenities. They do not appear to foster greed and over-consumption: for example, free access to museums or libraries does not lead to people rushing to these institutions to excess in order to develop one-upmanship over their neighbours. However, we can only approach such suggestions with a degree of scepticism. The use of public amenities is unlikely to be transferable unproblematically onto ownership of material goods.

This also raises further issues: is greed really only part of our character structure due to our economic system? Critics of such schemes would argue that because it is part of our human nature, a sane society along Fromm's recommendations would be doomed to fail. Then again, this position is also too easy. We already operate in most European societies a system of public amenities and at least subsidized access to education and health care. In the light of recent discussions regarding the health risks of childhood obesity, discussions around optimal consumption and the role of advertising have come into sharper focus.

How can such changes be realized more widely? Economic transformation, Fromm suggests, must come from two directions. The state needs to curb power of stockholders and management to limit the influence of profit motives. It also needs to be instrumental in establishing 'norms for healthy consumption'.[59] These changes have to be embraced by citizens who may even lead the way through consumer strikes. He gives the example of the power of consumers quite literally voting with their feet in refusing to buy private cars and using public transport instead in order to curtail the dominance of oil companies and the car industry.[60] In this area, however, consumer pressure has admittedly been modest. Then again, there are indeed some examples which show that consumer power can be instrumental in leading to saner production and consumption, as evident in recent moves towards Fair Trade and 'green' products.

For a humanistic development of the *arts*, Fromm recommends establishing a *'Supreme Cultural Council'* to offer advice to governments along the same lines as the US Food and Drug Administration. This body would consist of representatives of 'the intellectual and artistic elite'[61] including those holding opposing views on cultural issues. The notion of an 'elite' of this kind does, however, evoke concerns over taste dictatorship. This also comes across in his recommendations about literature where he distinguishes between 'escapist' and '"good" literature'.[62] Here, Fromm's ideas evoke an image of the paternalistic moralist stipulating what we should or should not read.

On the other hand, Fromm is not alone in his tightrope walk between limiting prescriptions and notions of individual freedom. Such tensions lie at the heart of any society which is run along liberal and social reformist values. Debates over how much the state should get involved in matters of 'taste' continue in democratic societies. For example, we regularly encounter situations in which one person's humour is seen as deeply offensive by another, leading to heated debates over censorship and freedom of speech. Of course such issues of interpretation will inevitably remain, even if we do follow Fromm's suggestions.

Political transformations

Fromm's main concern regarding political systems is the passivity of citizens and voters. His critique targets our *bureaucratic systems* which he regards as irresponsible in their objectification of people.[63] His point in highlighting how individuals – especially those in difficult circumstances – can become impersonal 'cases' in inflexible systems is indeed an important one. Arguably, since Fromm's times there have been changes in this respect. Professionals are trained and encouraged to respond to individual needs in nursing and social work education, although job rationalization and administrative pressures often work against putting these values into practice.

The other area in which he sees transformation as essential is our *democratic electoral system* which he regards as largely ineffective. Apathetic about their ability to bring about any changes, people lose interest and become passive, lost in complex mazes of political decision-making. Low election turnouts can be taken as an indication of an apathetic electorate.

His solution is to change 'a passive "spectator democracy" into an active "participatory democracy"'[64] and he sees decentralization and education as key elements for bringing about political transformation. He suggests that people need to be given adequate knowledge and feel that their decisions can have an effect. This would encourage individuals to re-engage with the system and exercise choice and agency in much more personalized and responsive ways, for example via 'participatory face-to-face groups'.[65] Such groups would be given factual information by individuals 'whose outstanding achievements and moral integrity are beyond doubt ... [forming] a non-political cultural agency'.[66] These groups would be able to vote on a number of issues, and their votes would be considered alongside those of 'universally elected representatives and a universally elected executive'.[67]

Globalization and One World politics

While Fromm may not have foreseen the precise economic and political intricacies of globalization, he certainly raised the need for a more global vision of solidarity:

> I believe that the One World which is emerging can come into existence only if a New Man comes into being – a man who has emerged from the archaic ties of blood and soil, and who feels himself to be the son of man, a citizen of the world whose loyalty is to the human race and to life, rather than to any exclusive part of it; a man who loves his country because he loves mankind, and whose judgement is not warped by tribal loyalties.[68]

In *To Have or To Be?* Fromm goes further in his concern with world economics and suggests that *'The gap between the rich and the poor nations must be closed.'*[69] He foresees catastrophic consequences if the status quo continues and the gap widens. Global unrest would ensue, affecting even those who believe themselves safe in the wealthy heartlands of Western civilization:

> famines will drive the population of the poor nations into such despair that they, perhaps with the help of sympathisers from the industrial world, will commit acts of destruction, even use small nuclear or biological weapons, that will bring chaos within the white fortress.[70]

Industrial nations, he suggests, must help to eliminate the conditions which cause famines and disease but without strings attached, and also without pressure to export the dictat of capitalism. As he says 'nothing is more telling about our selfishness than that we go on plundering the raw materials of the earth, poisoning the earth, and preparing nuclear war'.[71] These concerns in his later publications reflect the beginnings of 'green' thinking at the time, and his ideas were readily taken up by the 'alternative' movement in Europe and beyond. Although the need for change may have been there in the past, he addresses this issue with a renewed sense of urgency: 'Until now the One Man may have been a luxury, since the One World had not yet emerged. Now the One Man must emerge if the One World is to live.'[72] In an increasingly connected world, such visions are indeed essential, and Fromm was certainly right to point to these developments. In our times of global terrorism and climate change, Fromm's visions take on a new significance and poignancy.

Developing moral frameworks

With regards to the development of a moral framework, Fromm proposes a return to old rather than the creation of new values. He offers a historical analysis of how our evolving self-awareness and ensuing loss of a sense of union with nature left a void to be filled, which became populated with different notions of God according to how each culture interpreted its expression of the desire for security and unity. For example, patriarchal societies would see God as the all-seeing father and our task would be to please him and emulate the values he was thought to represent. Fromm suggests that the history of religion and philosophy can ultimately be seen as the history of the solutions people have put forward for dealing with our existential isolation. To him, the mature phase of the evolution of our spiritual development involved individuals taking on key values as intrinsic to their lives without the need to resort to an external god-figure of any kind – a final stage of development:

> from the beginning of the love for God as the helpless attachment to a mother Goddess, through the obedient attachment to a fatherly God, to a mature stage where God ceases to be an outside power, where man has incorporated the principles of love and justice into himself, where he has become one with God, and eventually, to a point where he speaks of God only in a poetic, symbolic sense.[73]

Based on his view of society's progress towards the rational, free individual, he proposes that the development of our rational humanistic conscience means that we will not need to defer to an external God-like source of morality in the future. He envisages that 'the theistic concepts are bound to disappear in the future development of humanity'.[74] Values like love and justice would then become our guiding principles due to their intrinsic importance and not because we fear that any transgressions will be punished in an afterlife. In tune with his condemnation of incestuous clinging to tradition, he regards beliefs in a paternalistic God-figure as a way in which we remain stuck in earlier, less developed, phases of religious maturity.

Fifty years later, Dawkins' analysis of the psychological foundations of religious faith examines similar concerns.[75] He suggests that there is indeed a need for us to find a frame of orientation but that filling this with notions of God prevents the development of other more appropriate humanistic and humanitarian ways of feeling connected.[76] Dawkins would regard *all* religions as absurd in promoting belief systems which do not link to scientific enquiry and in many cases were used to justify moral reasoning at odds with the values of Western liberal democracies. There may indeed be a psychological need for consolation and inspiration which religion has traditionally addressed but we have to recognize that our increased scientific understanding now calls for a rational examination of what he calls irrational beliefs. In his emphasis on reasoning and rationality, some similarities to Fromm's ideas are apparent.

However, Fromm's stance is rather more conciliatory in that he specifically highlights the ideals of religions as positive and emphasizes their humanistic commonalities. According to Fromm, humanistic ideals are already available in the fundamental beliefs underpinning different world religions and philosophies:

> We do not need new ideals or new spiritual goals. The great teachers of the human race have postulated the norms for sane living. ... In every center of culture, and largely without any mutual influence, the same insights were discovered, the same ideals were preached. We, today, who have easy access to all these ideas, who are still the immediate heirs to the great humanistic teachings, we are not in need of new knowledge of how to live sanely – but in bitter need of taking seriously what we believe, what we preach and teach. The revolution of our hearts does not require new wisdom – but new seriousness and dedication.[77]

When examining Fromm's references to different religious and philosophical thoughts, it is apparent that he wrote more about Judaism, Christianity and Buddhism than about Hinduism and Islam. He was, however, familiar with these religions, too, and counts them among his threads of wisdom and humanism.

He incorporated a prayer from the Upanishads (Hindu Sacred texts) into a daily ritual in his life. He and his wife would stand facing each other, hands on each others' shoulders, and recite a prayer for peace and harmony.[78] Fromm also saw Islam as built on a fundament of humanistic values of love and solidarity. This can be seen, for example, in his introduction to the Islamic mystic Rumi's work.[79] In the spirit of Fromm's own approach, further bridge-building has been attempted in this area. In 2007 the annual meeting of the International Erich Fromm Society took place in Morocco. Its focus was on dialogue between Islamist and Western ways of life, and several of its contributors highlighted similarities between Fromm's message of universal humanism and writers who interpret Islam in humanistic terms.[80] In Fromm's treatment of religion it is perhaps surprising, though, that he does not refer to the Bahá'í faith which explicitly shares his view of commonality between different religions (and Fromm's One World visions are acknowledged in this context[81]).

He observes that positive moral standards already run through society at a superficial level but that they are largely ineffective in channelling our actions. For example, societies may claim to follow Christian values, yet in the reality of everyday lives there is little evidence of the compassion and love which Jesus held up as the key principles for life guidance.

However, the reality of translating values into practice is complex. There are still many debates over the interpretation of what these great teachers said or meant. Many of their systems of thought were not entirely consistent even when seen in their own times. How exactly their messages should be brought forward to a different age remains open to debate. Catholicism, for example, can be seen as conservative, pro-establishment and anti-science in one place and as liberation theology in another. Fromm was aware of this and points to the difference between authoritarian and humanistic systems. This distinction cuts across different moral frameworks and can also be found *within* religions.

In his contemporary times, he argues, various stages of development were represented, reflecting aspects of the social structures of the time – some more forward thinking, others still anchored in answers which previous societies had constructed in response to our human need.[82]

Fromm described himself as 'not a theist or an atheist, but a non-theist'.[83] He had a deep interest in Western and Eastern religions but saw himself as having moved on from the stage of a theistic, historically constructed notion of God. He maintained some of his ethnic Jewishness like his enjoyment of its culture throughout his life. Yet this does not imply that he saw religion in the traditional sense as the source for life guidance. Drawing on Spinoza's views which regard God as an abstract notion of nature or life itself he claims that we can only find meaning within our own lives and relatedness: 'I believe that neither life nor history has an ultimate meaning ...Only man can find a goal for life and the means for the realization of this goal.'[84]

Nevertheless, Fromm at times remains close to religious language in his social analysis. For example, at the end of *The Sane Society* he predicts the arrival of a new universalistic 'religion' within the next few hundred years. It would embrace the humanistic teachings common to all great religions of the East and the West, aiming for advice on life guidance rather than doctrine, including new rituals conducive to the furthering of human solidarity. Fromm suggests that this new 'religion' cannot be 'invented. It will come into existence with the appearance of a great new teacher... In the meantime, those who believe in God should express their faith by *living* it; those who do not believe, by living the precepts of love and justice and – waiting.'[85] These points have a prophesizing ring to them, with Fromm almost adopting the role of St John in pointing to the Messiah yet to come.

Evaluating Fromm's view of society

What are we to make of Fromm's social critique? His formulations of 'the pathology of normalcy' and 'sane society' have undoubtedly played an important role in alerting us to the fact that a society's well-being need not correspond to its economic success. He has also made an important contribution in suggesting that personal well-being and social structures are closely linked and that improvement can only come about by focusing on both individual *and* social conditions.

Fromm paints a bleak picture of the psychological health of 20th century society in which our fundamental needs are ignored and distorted. Our only chance for improvement, he suggests, lies in drastic economic, political and cultural changes.

However, is Fromm's dreary picture justified? We can argue that a lack of focus on our needs for relatedness, identity and a frame of orientation have indeed contributed to a disintegration of the moral fabric of Western societies. A number of social scientists have taken this view in our time, and we will examine their ideas in Chapter 7. Yet, as already indicated, measures of national happiness or malaise are notoriously complex, and clear evidence for such links is difficult to muster. Acerbic critiques of the moral fabric of society have a long history, often reflected in the 'respectable fears' of the middle aged who look back with rose tinted spectacles on the supposed haleness of previous eras.[86]

Depending on where we look, we can see a picture of either decaying communities (for example high divorce rates) or of increasing human rights (for example patients' rights to access their health records). Furthermore, even those developments themselves can be assessed in different ways. High divorce rates can indicate personal unhappiness but can also show that communities are more willing to accept relationship breakdown which occurred in the past, too (though it was not acknowledged openly and often left individuals with no choice but to remain in destructive relationships). Increased patients' rights may signal acceptance of individuals' powers to make choices for themselves but can equally lead to less effective treatment if doctors make decisions based on fear of litigation rather than consideration of patients' health. A diagnosis of alienation and insanity at the societal level may thus be rather more complicated than Fromm presumes.

Similarly, the validity of Fromm's claim that his society consisted of a *majority* of alienated, passive automatons may depend on different perspectives. The existence of generations of concerned, responsible, caring and community-minded citizens speaks against his accusations. Whether they are in as small a minority as he suggests is impossible to verify. We must be open to the possibility that Fromm, having gained many of his insights into US society through clinical practice and the media (while he was living in Mexico), may have perceived a level of negativity uncharacteristic of its diversity.

In *The Sane Society*, Fromm at times comes up with what to the eye of the 21st century reader may look like moralistic tirades against Western capitalism. He certainly puts his cards on the table and asserts his views with the assurance of conviction: 'To speak of a "sane society" implies a premise different from sociological relativism. It ... implies that there are universal criteria for mental health which are valid for the human race as such, and according to which the state of health of each society can be judged.'[87] Linked to these claims is his idea that creating a sane society presents no more than technical problems, a challenge for future science: 'It is the task of the "science of man" to arrive eventually at a correct description of what deserves to be called human nature.'[88]

This is, however, problematic in a number of ways. First, as we have seen for his views on the needs of 'Man' outlined in Chapter 2, there is no clear evidence beyond his assertions that such needs (and resultant defence mechanisms) do in fact exist and that they are, as he suggests, common to us all. Second, the remedies which he proposes for the disease he diagnoses are also open to question. It would certainly be difficult to see *all* of his suggestions realized within anything resembling our current society. A number of difficult areas regarding his views on industrial relations have been outlined earlier.

Furthermore, Fromm's claim to have found the answer to society's problems is not exclusive to him. Politicians of all persuasions regularly roll out programmes which claim to do exactly what Fromm sets out to achieve – to improve our well-being and provide opportunities for work and a level of security and comfort. The question is how this can be realized in practice, and Fromm's view of humanistic communitarian socialism is only one of many solutions on offer. Those following more liberal views of economics would see business success as the answer to individual well-being. After all, one person's purchase of unnecessary consumer goods could mean that another's job is secure.

However, the question of how the economic growth through which capitalism defines its success is sustainable in the future is being asked increasingly in current times of financial insecurity[89] and environmental threat. Thus, a reminder of some of Fromm's ideas seems timely, and we will look at their continuing relevance in Chapter 7.

It is easy to be enthused by some of Fromm's ideas for a better society. The possibility of achieving at least some measure of 'humanness' in economic, political and cultural spheres cannot sound anything other than attractive. On the other hand, there is a sense of righteousness which sounds alien to our ears attuned to political critique and scepticism. He argues, for example, that with enough education, 'objective' information and the opportunity to reflect on values, people will 'naturally' make the 'right' decision – that is decisions matching his own humanistic vision.

As we have seen in Chapter 1, Fromm was suspicious of dogma and yet his own assertions at times come across as rather fixed and definite. As Ingleby puts it: 'Although Fromm is a staunch opponent of political centralism and totalitarianism, his own argument is curiously ethnocentric and coercive in nature.'[90] There is a paradox here in that Fromm preaches individualism and independence of herd conformity on the one hand but tries to convert us to his particular notion of humanism on the other. Then again, his directness can also be seen as a strength. In the intervening years since his publications, concerns about political spin have been raised frequently, and in this context his ideas come across as refreshingly direct proposals for discussion.

The direct nature of his advice is also what makes it so thought-provoking. For example, in the political sphere, he argues, there are 'only two camps: *those who care and those who don't care*'.[91] Perhaps this distinction can also be applied to people in society at a more general level. The question, then, is what we do if people don't care and don't want to care. It is perhaps because of perennial problems like this that Fromm is right in claiming that 'People today are yearning for human beings who have wisdom and convictions and the courage to act according to their convictions.'[92] In one sense he was certainly right: *To Have or To Be?* became a bestseller in Europe, and his readers appear to have cherished his call to reflection at the level of the individual and society even if his proposed changes were not all practicable. He has to be given credit for attempting to examine our social problems in such a wide ranging way and for having the courage to be openly political.

What makes Fromm's views on society – his analysis and suggestions for improvement – particularly interesting is that we can now view them with the benefit of some hindsight. Fifty years after the first publication of *The Sane Society* and thirty years after *To Have or To Be?* was published it is possible to look back over Fromm's predictions and suggestions and assess the extent to which his ideas may have been prescient and in what ways his proposals have been taken up in the 21st century. Chapter 7 will address the relevance of Fromm's work in this light.

6 Burning Boats or Building Bridges?

In Fromm's life story – both his personal and his professional paths – his intense and wide interest and involvement in many different aspects of human experience are striking. Not only did his life's journey take him to different countries and continents, it also bears witness to a man whose genuine curiosity in, and concern for, all things human made him reflect on, study and play an active part in a number of diverse areas, as we have seen in previous chapters. As Ingleby suggests: 'Fromm is an example of an increasingly scarce breed: a psychologist who wants to say something important about human life, and is willing to study beyond the limits of his discipline in order to get it right.'[1] Because this breadth particularly characterizes Fromm's work, we will use this chapter to examine its significance in a little more depth.

In relation to his therapeutic work Fromm is reported as saying that 'the patient must burn his bridges behind him before he can go forward'.[2] We can take this as an analogy of Fromm's own life. Leaving behind the orthodoxies of religion and psychoanalysis he moved forward to develop a wide-ranging and thought-provoking view of the human condition, the problems arising from its complexities and possible solutions. Should we see Fromm as a bridge builder who took our understanding towards new and more integrative and holistic approaches? Or did the range of his interests mean that his ideas fell between different disciplines relegating him on to the back benches of them all? In moving beyond rigid conceptual and methodological boundaries, did he burn his boats with the academic and psychoanalytic establishment?

There are arguments to be made for both of these positions, and this chapter aims to illuminate them.

Building bridges

Funk highlights two major threads running through Fromm's work. One is his attempt to specify the interaction between society and individual psyche. This brings together, for example in his notion of the 'social character', areas of study traditionally dealt with by different approaches: sociology and psychoanalysis. The second is his humanistic stance. This is reflected in his interest in the historical significance of humanistic values in religions and philosophies. In an interview for German radio, the 73-year-old Fromm described his attempts to fuse the values reflecting pre-bourgeois intellectual heritage with those aspects of the modern world which were dear to him. His aim was to imbue 'old' values with new meaning and to assert their significance in his society.[3]

Humanistic values are also the basis for the social changes which he advocates in his political activities. For example, in a speech which Fromm wrote for Eugene McCarthy's election campaign[4] he highlights the importance of reconciliation between different groups within the USA (when race and gender relations were high on the political agenda), between the USA and other countries (intense political conflict was rife: the Vietnam War and Cold War) and between rich and poor countries. Fromm sees a genuine commitment to the humanistic values of love, solidarity and justice as the foundation on which such bridges could be built.

Explorations of some of these combinations have already been mentioned in previous chapters. Here, we will look at three examples of bridge-building: his examination of Marx and Freud in *Beyond the Chains of Illusion* (1962), his attempt at bringing Buddhism and Psychoanalysis together and his combination of Meister Eckhart's and Marx's ideas in *To Have or To Be?*.

Linking Marx and Freud

Fromm starts *Beyond the Chains of Illusion* with what he calls an 'intellectual autobiography',[5] and Funk rightly describes this as his most 'personal' book.[6]

Fromm traces the beginnings of his interest in psyche and society to two experiences in his youth. The first one relates to a young female painter whose intense relationship with her father caused her to commit suicide when he died. Fromm found this preference for death in someone full of health and creativity incomprehensible, and he suggests that this was an impetus for his interest in Freud's theory when he encountered it as a young man.

His second formative experience was the upheaval of the First World War years which brought his questions about social issues to the fore. His concerns were linked to messianic prophecies of peace; of swords being turned into ploughshares.[7] He saw this reflected later on in some of Marx's visions for a more equal and harmonious society.

Fromm acknowledges fundamental differences between Freud and Marx in terms of what they see as our basic motivations: where the former emphasizes sexual drives, the latter regards socially fuelled greed for material objects as the driving force for behaviour. Each of these two thinkers has recommendations which lead to change and growth – of the person in one case, of society in the other. The call to look beyond the obvious and become aware of what is restricting our freedom is the common link between the two. 'Doubt and the power of truth and humanism are the guiding and propelling principles of Marx's and Freud's work.'[8]

With regards to Freud's ideas this means understanding our unconscious and accepting that what we assume to be our conscious motivations might in fact be a cover for very different processes deep in our psyches. Although Fromm disagrees with Freud over the idea that sexual energy should be seen as our main motivating force, he fully supports the notion of the liberating effect of insight.

According to Fromm, Marx revealed the importance of the economic structures and the fundamental inequalities between groups in society. In a capitalist system workers are exploited by their paymasters. A relentless drive to increase profits alienates them from the products of their hands. Production processes and technology – not human considerations – are taken as the starting point. Workers are also tied by the chains of their belief that they are powerless. Only when these dysfunctional relationships are exposed and workers become conscious of the common concerns of their class would people be able to overturn social structures and live in harmony in a socialist system.

Despite his respect for Freud's contribution in helping us to understand the unconscious he regards 'most of his applications of psychology to social problems … [as] … misleading constructions'.[9] For societal analysis, Fromm sees Marx's notions of socialism as particularly important but he highlights his disagreement with its interpretation in the Soviet context to which he refers as 'the vulgar forgery presented by Soviet communism'.[10] Instead, Fromm pins high hopes on the development of a global radical humanist movement. He looked with optimism to the development of his ideas and was in touch with many humanist socialist groups across the world.[11] In 1965 he published a collection of contributions from humanists from different countries, all united in a belief of the possibility that free, rational and loving individuals can live together in harmony in societies which are not bound by the rigid confines of communist states or illusions of freedom in psychologically empty consumerist societies.

In exposing illusory notions in the individual and society, both Freud and Marx were able to reveal what lies beneath the surface veneer of our everyday lives and its limiting effects on our development. Their common message was that holding onto 'false consciousness' keeps us in chains and prevents us from seeing things as they really are. These shackles had to be broken before full development of human powers could occur: for Freud, this meant overcoming neuroses, for Marx overturning an economic system which alienates us.

Fromm can thus be seen as a 'bridge builder' in his bringing together two of the most challenging thinkers of the 19th and early 20th century. Both of them have a huge influence on how we think of ourselves: Freud, in highlighting the unconscious aspects of mind and behaviour; Marx, in pointing to the fundamental importance of economic and social struc- tures. Fromm acknowledges the impact that both of these thinkers had on him, stating tellingly that standing on 'the shoulders of a giant like Freud one could see farther than the giant himself'.[12] Fromm claims that

> Different as they were, they have in common an uncompromising
> will to liberate man, an equally uncompromising faith in truth as the
> instrument of liberation and the belief that the condition for this
> liberation lies in man's capacity to break the chains of illusion.[13]

However, we can argue that Fromm's vantage point may obscure our under- standing in important aspects. After all, both Marx's and Freud's ideas have been attacked. Psychoanalysis has been termed a 'monumental sham'[14] by its critics; Freud's methods and assumptions have been questioned widely, as has the efficacy of his psychoanalytic interventions.[15] Although Marxism as a critique of capitalism has lived on beyond its founder, its translation into a socialist system as envisaged by Marx still awaits realization (even though many have tried!). We can also wonder to what extent we should go along with the 'truth' claims of either approach.

Fromm's attempt at creating a bridge between Marx and Freud certainly provides an impetus for further discussion. As Fromm himself admits, the difficulty lies in just how far we can go in looking for similarities. One major difference between the two thought systems is surely what they see as their goals, and Fromm does acknowledge this. He saw Freud as a 'liberal reformer' whose aim was to restore patients to their place and function in a society whose basic form he did not question. In contrast, 'Marx [was] a radical revolutionist'[16] who envisaged a major overturn of the socio-economic conditions which contribute to alienation and inequality. Viewed in this light, the link between the two may at times seem rather tenuous and leads us to cast doubt on how far such divergent thought systems can be brought together effectively.

Linking psychoanalysis and Buddhism

Humanistic values and the potential for change also underlie Fromm's endeavour to bring together psychoanalysis and Buddhism. His views are expressed in *Psychoanalysis and Zen Buddhism*, (1960) written for a workshop which Fromm organized in Cuernavaca, with D. T. Suzuki a major contributor.[17] Once again Fromm highlights the similarity between the two approaches in their concern for human well-being and their potential to lead to awareness and change.

The key aim of Buddhism is enlightenment. This includes conscious and intense experiencing of life in the 'here and now'. It also involves the practice of becoming free from attachment, overcoming greed. Self knowledge is an important aspect of this. However, Fromm emphasizes that this is not only intellectual knowing but a more encompassing experience which includes emotion and intuition. The focus is much more on 'being' and developing a respectful attitude towards oneself, others and the world.

Fromm claims that the aims of his version of psychoanalysis are very similar to those of Buddhism. The achievement of insight and enlightenment underpin both approaches. Through the process of psychoanalysis the individual achieves personal understanding. This allows her to recognize her unconscious motivations and move on from negativity towards a realization of her potential, freedom, happiness and love.[18] Another similarity between psychoanalysis and Buddhism is overcoming selfishness and greed and developing maturity, which, for Fromm, finds expression in compassion and love.

The aims of both perspectives can thus be seen as steps in what Suzuki calls 'the art of living'.[19] Just as psychoanalysis can be a way of achieving well-being and developing our biophilous productive potential, Buddhism emphasizes the Buddha-nature in all of us.[20] Furthermore, both approaches emphasize the importance of effective relationships: between analyst and patient and between Zen master and pupil, respectively.

How useful is this assumption of a connection between Buddhism and Fromm's humanistic psychoanalysis? We could argue that some of the links come across as rather far-fetched and contrived. There are, after all, important differences. Funk[21] suggests that Buddhism's aim towards transcendence and 'nothingness' would not seem to sit well alongside Fromm's call for reason and love. Furthermore, Buddhism – a religion – aims to provide for its believers a framework of making sense of life and death. In contrast, psychoanalysis, at least in its original inception, developed as a therapeutic approach. Perhaps Fromm's version of psychoanalysis (with its emphasis on life guidance) does indeed take on qualities of a religion, moving it into a realm which goes beyond its original scope. In fact, some of Freud's critics[22] have argued that even *his* views resemble a religion rather than a science (Freud saw his own approach as scientific). In this sense the bridge between Buddhism and psychoanalysis is perhaps appropriate. Fromm certainly succeeds in bringing to light some of these potential similarities – in particular the essential role of awareness and self-knowledge – in both systems of thought.

Linking Meister Eckhart and Karl Marx

In *To Have or to Be?* Fromm explores links between what seem at first sight radically different perspectives: Meister Eckhart's and Karl Marx's. The connection between a medieval mystic and a 19th century economist may seem particularly obscure, especially since Marx is well known for his disdain for religion.

However, Fromm challenges our simplistic notion of Marx's views on religion and argues that the oft quoted 'opium of the people' phrase needs to be understood in the context of Marx's views of the human condition in a more general sense. For the pain sufferer who takes opium, the key issue is the pain, without which there would be no need for the drug.[23] In Marx's view we turn to religion as the opium because our deficient social conditions generate this need. Therefore, our main focus should be on ways of addressing the pain resulting from exploitative societies. The solution to the root problem lies in creating a society based on a way of human relating in which envy and greed are absent. As we have seen earlier, Fromm traces this notion of a harmonious and equal society back to the Old

Testament prophets and their utopian promises. Marx, like Fromm, appears to have had a penchant for their proclamations,[24] though both Marx and Fromm saw the development towards equality and harmony as a historical process rather than the promise of a metaphysical event. Fromm agrees with Marx that a society in which such human relating is possible would need to be based on principles radically different from capitalist systems in which money and property appear to define individuals and human bonds.

To illuminate our understanding of the dysfunctional nature of what he perceived his contemporary society to be and what he saw as the way forward, Fromm points to Meister Eckhart's notions of 'having' and 'being'. In their essence, these terms map neatly onto Marx's views of alienating capitalism on the one hand and his vision for socialism on the other.

Meister Eckhart's idea of *having* describes constraints linked to greed and envy. We want to own and possess material goods, knowledge or other people to such an extent that we lose our individuality and become possessed by owning. Since we define ourselves by 'having' we are never satisfied but, envious of others who 'have' more, become driven by the 'having' mode which permeates our whole attitude to life.[25] Fromm thought that Eckhart's notion was applicable to the individual and also characterized the main thrust of Western post-war society. It describes a meaningless striving for accumulating more and more possessions to fill the emptiness caused by a lack of real purpose in life.

In contrast, *being* 'denotes the unfolding of our full potential and freedom from illusion'. For Eckhart the basis for the 'being' mode is the socially altruistic, awake and aware person. Although Marx focused mainly on economic analysis, similarities to Eckhart's views are apparent in Marx's notion of the productive and active person in an unalienating work environment. Parallels to Fromm's idea of the 'productive character' (see Chapter 2) are also obvious. In *To Have or To Be?* he develops 'being' and its focus on the active, compassionate and caring individual as the blueprint for a better society with sane production and consumption patterns (see also Chapter 5).

Should we see such juxtapositions as a brilliant way of highlighting a common humanistic thread between great thinkers which can provide the foundation for the analysis of modern societies? Or do such efforts result in a stilted combination of essentially different thought systems which do not do justice to key aspects of either? As Chaudhuri[26] suggests, Fromm sidesteps one of Marx's central ideas – that of class struggle. He thus presents us with a rather emasculated version of Marxism, which attracted criticism from the ranks of more radical Marxists. On the other hand, bringing together key features from both thinkers in 'being' versus 'having' can provide a useful tool for individual and social analysis.

A bridge too far?

In a number of his publications, for example *The Sane Society* and *To Have or To Be?*, Fromm attempts to trace humanistic values across various different belief systems. He claims support for his formulations for a healthy orientation to life from the writings of 'the great Masters of Living'[27] including, for example, Buddha, Jesus, Meister Eckhart, the Hebrew prophets, Sigmund Freud and Karl Marx.[28]

Whether this argument can be sustained or whether this is a bridge too far, is a matter of debate. Commenting on the 1991 re-publication of *The Sane Society*, Ingleby suggests that this attempt to bring different viewpoints together leads to a rather paradoxical position: Fromm 'argues for freedom, but makes one particular version of it – his own – compulsory. Buddha, Christ, Lao Tsu and Mohammed must all lie down on the procrustean bed of liberalism and individualism, and any culture which does not enshrine these Western European ideals is diagnosed as "underdeveloped" or "ill-adapted to human nature".'[29]

However, although Ingleby's criticism is well put, we could argue that this problem runs deeper. Since the messages of the major world religions are linked to the societal conditions within which they were formulated, interpretation of, for example, Jewish, Christian or Muslim beliefs in the context of 21st century societies continues to occupy Rabbis, Ministers and Imams as well as their followers.

Then again, perhaps Fromm's observation that at least *some* messages of humanism appear to be shared among the major world religions with comforting regularity represents a much needed conciliatory way forward. We will examine this possibility in more depth in Chapter 7.

Burning boats

We have already noted in previous chapters that Fromm distanced himself from a number of different academic orientations. Although he was very

open to different disciplines and their ways of studying the human condition he did not really fit comfortably into any one particular area in the
academic landscape of his time. Disagreements occurred, for example, with
aspects of traditional psychoanalysis, mainstream psychology and humanistic psychology.

Psychoanalysis

Fromm moved away from traditional Freudian approaches in a number of
ways. In Chapter 2 we saw how Fromm took the paradox of our existence
and our relatedness to the world as his starting point. This contrasts
significantly with Freud's emphasis on sexual drives. In relation to expla-
nations of aggression Freud proposes a destructive 'death instinct'. Fromm
is critical of this and suggests that creativeness and destructiveness both
stem from our existential needs: destructive negativity occurs when opportunities for creativity are not available. Fromm is also sceptical of Freud's
evidence base and suggests that his notion of the 'death instinct' was 'based
on rather abstract speculations and offers hardly any convincing *empirical
evidence*'.[30] However, as we have seen, this criticism applies to some of
Fromm's work, too.

In Chapter 4 we examined how Fromm also turned away from some of
the key principles of Freud's therapeutic approach. He questions the value
and efficacy of Freud's set-up in which the analyst is a largely silent listener
with the patient prostrate on a couch. Instead, Fromm turns the therapist
role into a much more directive one with the patient facing the analyst.
In view of these differences from traditional psychoanalysis, psychoanalytic institutions in turn became wary of Fromm (see also Chapter 1).

'Purist' psychoanalysts regarded Fromm's ideas as heretically revision-
ist, and, as a result, his recognition in more traditional psychoanalytic literature is modest. Bacciagaluppi[31] suggests that this is due to him moving
further towards radical humanistic leanings rather than the rarity of his
writing on psychoanalytic technique. Fromm himself appears to have mirrored these reservations. He seems not to have followed too closely the
more recent developments in psychoanalysis during his lifetime.[32]

Despite differences and disagreements, Fromm aligned himself with
Freudian principles. When asked to elaborate on the main difference
between his own and Freud's ideas, he replied: 'I consider myself ... as a
Freudian who tries to develop Freud's theory on the basis of new clinical

findings and of a different philosophical approach to the problem of human nature. Freud's approach was that of the mechanistic materialism prevalent at the end of the last century.'[33] This prompted a focus on drives and their satisfaction. Fromm, in contrast, focuses on our existential needs.

There is also evidence that he maintained deep admiration for Freud. For example, he appears to have returned to reading Freud every time he started to write a new paper. Those who knew Fromm personally remember how respectful Fromm seems to have been of Freud.[34] Burston refers to the reverence for Freud expressed in Fromm's writings and exchanges with colleagues as an example of what he terms 'Freud piety'.[35]

Looking at more recent academic developments in areas related to psychoanalysis, we see attempts, for example by Hollway and Jefferson,[36] to bring together exactly some of the elements which were important to Fromm. Similar to Fromm's approach,[37] interpretative methods are used to examine individuals' responses in terms of their unconscious meanings and their relationship to social processes. However, Fromm's work is not mentioned by them.

Chrzanowski suggests that Fromm himself may not have been too worried about such omissions:

> His influence on current analytic thinking often goes unacknowledged – and despite whatever aspects of narcissism may have fueled some of his preoccupations – I have been left to conclude that he would be pleased that he has not become an icon and instead has had a wide spread influence on our theory and practice.[38]

This may be the case – yet it seems a pity that his work is not used more explicitly and acknowledged for its influence.

Thus we gain the impression that Fromm's place was somehow not quite in the inner circle of psychoanalysts yet he was also not prepared to turn his back on psychoanalysis altogether.

Mainstream psychology

One approach, however, which Fromm rejects almost wholeheartedly, is Skinnerian[39] behaviourism. It attempts to explain behaviour with reference to reinforcement properties in the environment. Put very simply, behaviourists assume that behaviour will be repeated if rewards ensue; if punishment or no reward follows a particular behaviour, its repetition is thought to be less likely. Fromm's assessment of Skinner was rather unflattering: 'Basically, Skinner is a naïve rationalist who ignores man's passions.'[40] He did not address those issues which Fromm saw as important – for example love, solidarity and relatedness – because they were not amenable to the experimental studies which behaviourists regarded as of the essence in the scientific study of psychology. Fromm derides 'Skinnerism [as] the psychology of opportunism dressed up as new scientific humanism.'[41] He is particularly critical of behaviourism's lack of focus on personal and social meanings which he sees as essential to a full understanding of our existence.

These criticisms need to be understood in the context of the history of psychology. Rejecting Freudian assertions about the unconscious as untestable and not amenable to scientific research, behaviourism saw its star ascending in academic psychology departments from roughly the 1930s till the 1970s. In its attempt to emulate a traditional natural science approach it concentrated only on those aspects of (often animal) behaviour which could be tested in controlled experimental study. The scientific method became the new straightjacket of psychology. This may have helped its aspirations to the high status afforded the natural sciences in our society but meant that for a while the most human aspects of our experience were seen as no longer part of its subject matter.

Fromm was certainly aware of this and in *The Anatomy of Human Destructiveness* he criticizes laboratory based experimental methods in psychology as inadequate:

> Psychology seems to have wanted to attain respectability by imitating the method of the natural sciences, albeit those of fifty years ago. ... Furthermore, the lack of theoretical significance is often covered up by impressive-looking mathematical formulations which are not germane to the data and do not add anything to their value.[42]

Even though Fromm often emphasizes the need for 'scientific' understanding, he is sceptical of the value of knowledge gained via experimental manipulation of variables in psychology laboratories. He criticizes Stanley Milgram's[43] well known study of obedience in which experimental subjects were instructed by an authority figure to give what they thought were electric shocks up to potentially lethal levels to another person, a confederate of the experimenter (in reality the set-up was fake and nobody was hurt!). This was to show how ordinary people would be capable of harming, even potentially killing, others when instructed to do so by a person in authority, with assumed parallels to the behaviour shown by, for example, guards in Nazi concentration camps. Fromm questions in what ways an artificial psychology laboratory can offer us any in depth understanding about such situations. He regards looking directly at real life events as a far superior method in giving us meaningful insights and refers, for example, to Bettelheim's insider studies of the dynamics of behaviour in concentration camps.[44]

This may illustrate what Billig describes as Fromm's 'intellectual contortions in his book *The Anatomy of Human Destructiveness*, to avoid mentioning experimental results'.[45] However, Billig's assessment is perhaps not entirely fair: Fromm appears happy to accept experimental evidence when it relates to biological functions which relate to our experience – for example brain cell activity.[46] Fromm's objections seem to be towards those studies which assume that behaviours shown under abstracted laboratory conditions can help us to understand the complexity of our real-life experience.

> I believe that the exploration of aggression either in the laboratory of the psychoanalytic interview or in a socially given 'laboratory' is, from a scientific standpoint, much preferable to the methods of the psychological laboratory, as far as analysis of behaviour is concerned; however, it requires a much higher level of complex theoretical thinking than do even very clever laboratory experiments.[47]

It seems that to Fromm, 'science' means exploring the complexities of life rather than adhering to particular methods which may obscure rather than promote such understanding.

Thirty years on, Milgram's studies are now seen as classic, and are almost ubiquitous in social psychology textbooks. In contrast, Fromm's fame appeared to wane towards the end of the 20th century, and this is perhaps not surprising, given the prominence of the experimental method in many prestigious psychology departments (though this is now more focused on cognitive processes rather than purely behaviour). Pronouncements like: 'Psychology as a science has its limitations, and, as the logical consequence of theology is mysticism, so the ultimate consequence of psychology is love'[48] must have been anathema to supporters of Skinnerian behaviourist rat experiments in Fromm's day. It would seem no surprise that due to his methodological and ethical objections to studying people in this way, no welcome would be extended to him from these quarters.

This is also illustrated by Frie's explanation for Fromm's relative obscurity in academic sociology departments: 'Fromm was considered one of those "fuzzy" European thinkers whose interests were commonly derided as not sufficiently Anglo-Saxon in nature.'[49] Paradoxically, Fromm's very success with mass audiences and readerships may have contributed to this. Frie surmises that according to the prejudices of established academia 'no serious academic could ever hope, or would ever aspire, to sell his or her writings on such a large scale. Bestsellers were the death knell of a true academic.'[50]

Fromm's strong attacks on mainstream psychology may explain why his place in academia is generally modest. There are few discussions of his ideas in textbooks and journals subscribing to the still dominant experimental paradigm.

Humanistic psychology

One approach within psychology which shares Fromm's scepticism about experimental behaviourism and orthodox psychoanalysis is humanistic psychology. This is often called the 'third force' to describe its move away from the assumption that either environmental contingencies or the unconscious *determine* who we become. Humanistic psychologists claim that people also need to be seen as capable of choice and self-direction. We might expect Fromm to find a place in their midst. However, as we have seen in Chapter 4, Fromm was careful to distance himself from this approach which was largely dominated by the writings of Abraham Maslow and Carl Rogers.

Rogers himself highlights parallels between Fromm's and his own view of our isolation in the context of modern society and of, for example, the alienating effects of modern entertainment.[51] However, as we noted in Chapter 4, Fromm viewed Rogers' ideas about 'client-centred' counselling as inflated, since he regards *all* therapy as essentially client centred. He felt that a counselling approach which proceeded at the pace of clients' own self-discovery was needlessly drawn out. Furthermore, it ignored the importance of the unconscious which Fromm still saw as an essential aspect of understanding the human condition.

Nonetheless, we can certainly trace similarities between Fromm's and Rogers' approach in the shift towards humanistically informed therapies and counselling. Both Fromm and Rogers also made the fundamental assumption that the client himself must be seen as ultimately capable of autonomy and responsible for his own actions – including his part in the therapeutic relationship.

Fromm acknowledges Maslow's contribution to our understanding of human needs: Maslow's 'pyramid of needs' specifies physiological, and aesthetic needs, and needs for safety, belonging, love, esteem and self-actualization. Fromm concedes that there are similarities between Maslow's and his own views of human needs but criticizes Maslow's ideas as unsystematic and lacking in an examination of their origins in existential dilemmas.[52] In this sense, Fromm is to be seen not as a humanistic psychologist but as someone who approaches psychology from a fundamentally humanist psychoanalytic orientation.

Fromm also emphatically distanced himself from the burgeoning self discovery and personal development mass market of his time. This is perhaps rather ironic since book sales in this area no doubt contributed to fuelling Fromm's own success and turned his works into bestsellers. He had originally planned to end *To Have or To Be?* with a chapter offering concrete suggestions for applying his principles of a 'being' orientation to our everyday lives. This was to comprise ideas on how to practise concentration, meditation and self-analysis in order to develop a more awake and aware approach to life (published in 1989 as *The Art of Being*[53]). Yet he decided not to include this, concerned that his ideas might be misunderstood as suggesting that the problems of human existence could be solved just by self-analysis and self-discovery. His fear was that this would sideline his critique of social, political and economic systems[54] and might reduce his social concerns to purely psychological issues.[55]

Bridges to future enquiry

How did Fromm's oscillating position between different thought systems fit into the landscape of diverse approaches in Fromm's time? *The Anatomy of Human Destructiveness,* first published in 1973, shows particularly clearly how Fromm attempted to bring together various methods of enquiry in order to gain a more holistic, comprehensive account of the role of aggression in the human condition. He was not afraid to step outside the comfort zone of his own discipline, and approached experts in the fields of neuro-anatomy and neurophysiology to teach him what he needed to know about their fields of expertise. When working on this book – by then in his seventies – Fromm found ingenious ways of exchanging knowledge: 'for each lesson he received he would offer an hour of psychoanalytic supervision to his teacher'.[56]

The diversity of disciplines on which he draws also illustrates how psychology itself occupies a fluid and at times contradictory position between science and philosophy. Fromm's breadth of interests can be seen to highlight division and divisiveness between different approaches.

He certainly emphasizes the potential enrichment which different disciplines can offer to each other:

> Each science, neurophysiology as well as psychology, has its own method and necessarily will deal with such problems as it can handle at a given point in its scientific development. It is the task of the psychologist to challenge the neurophysiologist, urging him to confirm or deny his findings, just as it is his task to be aware of neurophysiological conclusions and to be stimulated and challenged by them.[57]

Whatever weaknesses we may want to highlight about Fromm's approach, his analysis of the human condition is to be commended for not shying away from the complexities of our existence. In this sense he was certainly very much a bridge builder, keen to study and bring together the diverse features which weave the fabric of our lives.

Based on his analysis of existential needs Fromm derives specific recommendations regarding how individuals can make their lives more meaningful. He also examines what social changes are necessary to make this possible and thus prevent the occurrence of malignant aggression. These areas of moral principles and life guidance are commonly discussed in the context of philosophy, and it comes as no surprise that Aristotle and Spinoza are among Fromm's sources of inspiration for an analysis of existential needs and their implications.

However, Fromm refers to psychology as a *science* in whose name certain generalizations are possible and desirable: 'Human nature, though being the product of historical evolution, has certain inherent mechanisms and laws, to discover which is the task of psychology.'[58] He is optimistic about the success of finding generally valid principles:

> the state of well-being of man can be described as empirically and objectively as the state of ill-being; conditions conducive to

well-being can be ascertained, as can those leading to ill-being, both physical and mental. A study of the system Man can lead to the acceptance of objectively valid values, on the ground that they lead to the optimal functioning of the system or, at least, that if we realize the possible alternatives, the humanistic norms would be accepted ... by most sane people.[59]

This also points to the very paradox with which psychology and other disciplines grapple: although we share some features of our common humanity with all other human beings, we are at the same time unique. Starting life with a complex mix of genetic and evolutionary propensities, we add to this a colourful cocktail of personal and social meanings as we grow up, sharing some features with others yet experiencing ourselves as one of a kind in our individuality. Such complexities do not go down well with narrow methodologies and are seldom addressed directly as part of psychology.

One notable exception to this is Stevens' trimodal theory[60] which presents a framework attempting to integrate the study of different aspects of our existence such as biological, symbolic meanings and our capacity for self-awareness and reflection. In particular, he argues that different epistemologies (or forms of understanding and methods) will be required for effective understanding of these aspects. He distinguishes, for example, between the methods of natural science appropriate for biological investigation and interpretative or hermeneutic methodologies which are essential for understanding meanings.

Further links *between* disciplines have also been made. Publications attempting to build bridges between brain study, philosophy and psychology have increasingly populated bookshelves. Writers like Damasio[61] and Zeki[62] have explored ways in which we can gain more wide-ranging understanding of complex experiences like emotions and consciousness by bringing together biological science, psychology and philosophy. Links have also been made between philosophy and psychology exploring meeting points between existentialist philosophy and psychology, in particular in psychotherapy.[63] Further fruitful alliances arise from links between poetry and therapy.[64] It is possible that such approaches will help to provide a more integrated view. However, divisions between different disciplines may mean that the concerns which Fromm raises as central to our human experience continue to be caught between sociology, psychology, philosophy, art and science.

As we have seen, the very breadth of his analysis may have cost Fromm an assured place in the Valhalla of academic or psychoanalytic thinkers (at least for the time being). However, it could also be argued that any account of the human condition which only concentrates on one aspect of it cannot possibly provide credible understanding. In this sense, Fromm's contribution can be seen as an important step forward in tackling the complexities and paradoxes of the human experience head on. Perhaps he himself did not quite build the bridges which are necessary in order to bring different approaches together but he certainly points us to the need to be aware of other positions and not to remain stuck in narrow dogmatic niches.

As Ingleby suggests:

Fromm 'has never really been granted the academic recognition which he deserves. His most striking characteristic, his ability to draw upon and combine several different disciplines, is precisely what has got him into trouble with the specialized practitioners of these disciplines. For psychoanalysts, he is too "sociological"; for sociologists, too "essentialist"; for Marxists, too "voluntaristic"; for theologians, too "humanist". Precisely because he mixes so many discourses and cuts across so many disciplines, he has tended to be marginalized by all of them.'[65]

Fromm himself was reluctant to be tied down to particular dogmas or schools of thought. For him, burning boats and leaving behind the established and familiar was to be seen as a liberating experience which paved the way for new ways of exploring the age old territory of the nature of human existence. His breadth of approach has much to commend itself: we need those bridges between different disciplines to establish a more rounded and convincing picture of what it is to be human; and to derive from this constructive ways of dealing with the dilemmas which inevitably arise from the human condition.

7 The Relevance of Fromm's Ideas in Our Time

The previous chapters have given an outline of some of Fromm's work. As we have seen, his ideas were extremely popular in their heyday. What has become of them since? Are they still meaningful in our times? This chapter will try to trace the relevance of Fromm's ideas in current social trends and analysis. To pull the threads of different facets of Fromm's work together, we will begin with a brief overview of previous chapters.

Chapter 1 gave a résumé of some of the key aspects of Fromm's life and the socio-cultural context of his time. His life path was characterized by loss and upheaval but also by love and creativity. Themes of individual autonomy and a search for meaning and for positive relatedness are apparent in his development. Chapter 2 discussed Fromm's view of what it is to be human. A key point is the *paradox of our existence*: we are at the same time part of nature in our embodiment and yet we transcend it by the power of our self-awareness. In the absence of direction from biological instincts we have to create our own meaning and purpose both at an individual and a social level.

His emphasis on *mature and productive love* as a way of dealing with these tensions was highlighted in Chapter 3 which examined Fromm's view of personal relationships. Individuality, love and solidarity are some of the main ways in which he suggests our existential needs can be addressed.

Chapter 4 showed how his views of the *therapeutic relationship* have moved from Freudian psychoanalysis to a more humanistic approach to therapy, reflected in his writing and psychoanalytic practice. The quality of the therapist-patient relationship in 'face-to-face' relating lies at the heart of his method.

Fromm's assessment of the *individual in society* was the focus of Chapter 5. It also dealt with his analysis of how his contemporary consumerist society with its emphasis on a 'having' orientation fails the very essence of our human existence. His suggestions for improvement include a call for humanistic communitarian socialism with proposals for national and international transformations of economic, social and cultural practices.

Chapter 6 mapped Fromm's ideas onto the wider intellectual context of developments in psychology and psychotherapy. It suggested that while his range of interests may have meant that his ideas have never fully found a home in one single topic or area of enquiry, they point to interesting ways of building bridges between different disciplines in order to advance our understanding of the human condition.

This final chapter, while acknowledging some of the criticisms which can be levelled at Fromm's work, will show how a number of his thoughts can be seen as highly relevant to the world in which we now live.

What are Fromm's ideas worth?

As we have seen in the preceding chapters, Fromm's ideas are intriguing and thought-provoking, often striking in their clarity and plausibility. There is no denying Fromm's importance as a key thinker of the 20th century. In Chapters 1 and 6 we noted that his fame, though waxing and waning in different areas of social critique and psychology, is clearly illustrated in his bestsellers and his popularity across the world. However, at times Fromm's points appear to raise more questions than they answer.

Fromm's ideas on the social character constitute an interesting attempt to bring together a focus on the individual and on society. His concepts are helpful in highlighting changing patterns in society such as, for example, his notion of a 'marketing character' which no longer has a stable sense of his or her own values but instead tries to fit into any particular niche that seems attractive. However, although his empirical work on the social character goes some way towards providing more concrete substantiation for his ideas, we are generally expected to accept them on the basis of their plausibility.

To what extent we regard Fromm's evidence base as problematic is closely tied to our own expectations. If psychology is to be seen as a discipline akin to the natural sciences, many of Fromm's ideas will come across as unsubstantiated. If, on the other hand, we see its role in providing insight, wisdom and life guidance, his theories and concepts will be seen to provide at the very least a starting point for further discussion. In common with those whose ideas have influenced him, like for example Marx, Freud,

Spinoza and Meister Eckhart, Fromm's appeal lies in inspiration rather than quantification.

Was Fromm right in assuming that the essence of the human condition can be traced back to the core existential issue; that is our struggle with the paradox of being part of nature in our embodiment and yet transcending it through our self-awareness? And does the answer to this challenge really lie in developing productive relating, underpinned by a loving orientation to others and to life itself? These issues raise deeply complex and philosophical questions about what we take as our basic values in life.

Humanistic ideals also underlie his social critique urging us to awake from illusion and change our ways. His analysis is accompanied by suggestions of how we should transform aspects of our society to make it more conducive to human needs. His commitment to humanistic communitarian socialism comes across strongly. However, his suggestions for improvement at times sound naïve and overly general, paying less attention, for example, to the complexities of world economics. His insistence on simultaneous fundamental changes in economic, political and cultural realms certainly seems a tall order, in that his suggestions gnaw away at the very essence of our Western and arguably global system of capitalism.

Fromm himself follows a rather mixed path, borrowing concepts from diverging ideologies. On occasions he calls for social reformist state intervention to curb the inhumane excesses of a liberal market economy. Then again he demands individual freedom associated with liberalist ideologies which do not favour what they would regard as state interference. At times his ideas follow a conservative ideology which recommends wholesome entertainment and he extols the virtues of patience and respect in relationships. On other occasions, he borrows from Marxism to advocate some radical changes in society. This makes for a rather colourful and at times conflicting amalgam of suggestions associated with very different thought systems.

However, he is not alone in this balancing act. Many countries in the Western world are not following a path of unfettered free market economies but governments keep some checks on market processes in order to protect their citizens. The balance between personal freedom and the ways in which states should intervene to support individuals through educational, health and social provisions continues to lie at the heart of many political debates in Western democracies. Fromm's emphasis on solidarity and community activism is an important message to remind us that the key features of the human values of respect, care and concern need to underlie the way in which we organize our lives economically, politically and socially. This is particularly important in times when inequalities are increasing.[1] Even if Fromm's ideas do not find their way into the heart of all policies, they provide a counterbalance to the messages of capitalist excess; its inequalities and potential psychological emptiness.

From whichever angle we approach Fromm's work, it appears to lead us to his humanistic message which emphasizes the commonality of existential issues and suggests that the paradox between individuality and connectedness can be solved through productive relating with others. Wilde's assessment seems very apt in this context: 'Fromm is unique among social scientists of the late twentieth century in offering a thoroughly worked-out and well-defended view of human essence as a philosophical grounding for an appeal for solidarity.'[2]

While the edifice of Fromm's notion of unifying humanism appears impressive, the cohesiveness of its foundations could be called into question. He often repeats or rewords his main message in order to persuade us of the importance of individual and social choices in favour of life, love and productive relating. It remains debatable whether the humanistic values whose ubiquity he proclaims can be traced across different thought and belief systems quite as unproblematically as he suggests. As we have seen in Chapters 5 and 6, his proclamation of a clear thread of humanism running through the major world religions and philosophies can be seen to be based on a rather biased selection from these sources.

Furthermore, Fromm's ideals are slippery customers. When we look at attempts to translate them into life guidance they range from the intensely personal to the realms of One World politics, from change achieved by personal effort to recommendations for an overhaul of our entire system. This leaves Fromm open to being pigeonholed as either a kind of Hippie guru of yesteryear or else an airy-fairy utopian whose ideas take us to the realm of impossibility. Neither of these clichés is true or fair. Fromm's deeply held values of our common humanity are important messages to take forward into the 21st century. While we may not agree with all of the implications Fromm drew from them, they are at the very least an essential *counterpoint* to some alienating and potentially destructive developments in our society. They provide a way of deepening our understanding of the human condition and point to some constructive ways forward.

Fromm's ideas in the 21st century

What we can make of Fromm's ideas in our times? As we will discuss below, many of his views can be applied to current trends in Western society. Some of the suggestions which Fromm made 25 or 50 years earlier have indeed been taken up, others still await realization or have moved off the agenda altogether. In some areas Fromm's predictions of how society would evolve have turned out almost prophetic, in other fields what he foresaw did not materialize. However, as Wilde asserts, many of his suggestions for change 'retain a direct relevance to our present situation and promote an ethical approach which asks how people can promote processes and structures consonant with a more humane and productive life'.[3] As the following examples will highlight, a particular strength in Fromm's approach is his attempt to bring together different strands of influence. Individual problems are linked to their societal context; social concerns are explored in terms of what individuals can do to change unproductive lifestyles and damaging social structures.

Mental health and happiness in contemporary society

Fromm claims that a sense of isolation, alienation, and lack of productive relatedness is characteristic of his society. It is also one of the often neglected reasons for negativity, destructiveness and violence:

> One of the most important – and least studied – is, in my opinion, the boredom, the powerlessness, the isolation, the inner sense of being lost that beset man in industrialized society ... it arises from the feeling of having lost one's direction, one's values, the sense of being guided from within, by one's conscience ... The individual feels he is a nobody, that he has lost his control over the things, the institutions and the circumstances which he himself has created. It brings on a sense of separation from others and from himself, a lack of joy and, finally, an indifference to life itself – his own life and that of others.[4]

Further more recent research has lent credence to these points. For example, *Self Determination Theory* covers issues which parallel Fromm's concerns. It puts forward the idea that the extent to which basic psychological needs are met will give us an indication of a person's well-being. A proposed list of needs is similar to Fromm's – competence, relatedness and autonomy[5]

– though he is not cited in this. *Self Determination Theory* claims to look at individuals in their social environments. However, it stops short at the openly political implications which Fromm derives from his existential needs. His suggestions go beyond a focus on the individual and encourage us 'to build a society in which there is greater possibility to practice love and integrity, a society which functions in the name of life'.[6]

Similar points apply to another area which has examined mental health concerns: 'positive psychology' as outlined, for example, by Seligman. His earlier work helped to identify that thought patterns characterized by a sense of helplessness and a feeling of not being able to exert any control over life circumstances seem to be connected to the incidence of depression.[7] We can assist individuals to change such patterns through interventions like Cognitive Behavioural Therapy. Seligman (and others) have followed this up with a more explicit focus on positive aspects of our experience – such as happiness. Drawing on the same sources which Fromm examined five decades earlier, they, too, point to the ubiquity of certain virtues in different religions and philosophical systems of thought (though it seems that in their attempt to develop a 'scientific' approach, Fromm's ideas have been largely overlooked). These virtues include 'wisdom and knowledge, courage, love and humanity, justice, temperance and spirituality and transcendence'.[8] At first glance, similarities to Fromm's approach appear obvious.

The 'happiness' and 'well-being' agenda promoted by positive psychology writers has been addressed in the UK nationally with Layard's call for improved mental health provisions aiming to help people with such coping strategies.[9] However, opinions diverge as to how much focus should be on the individual – such as the availability of treatment – or on a more openly political agenda. Clark makes this point. His call for an 'Erich Fromm party' highlights the importance of considering mental health as a political issue.[10] He criticizes Layard's emphasis on individually based therapies. Treating individuals to make them think happy thoughts and encouraging them to harbour illusions about negative life situations would seem to go against more meaningful change on a wider level. (It should be noted, however, that Layard has recently promoted policies for change which include values (love and respect) echoing Fromm's ideas. His examination of the negative effects of excessive individualism, social inequality and decline in trust follows closely some of Fromm's social concerns. Although Layard and Dunn[11] do not refer to Fromm directly, their critical analysis of childhood in contemporary society shows clear parallels to his work, demonstrating once again its relevance in our time.)

Similar criticisms are made by The Midlands Psychology Group in the UK who suggest that the current emphasis on 'happiness' amounts

> at best to a naïve attempt to improve the world through wishful thinking, and at worst to a form of insidious social control ... What we need to develop is a greater ability to help people to place their distress firmly in a social and material context, and to articulate their experience of their world – including its potential for pain – as the first step toward trying to make that world a more tolerable place in which to live. This is essentially a political task.[12]

It would seem likely that Fromm would welcome such critical comments.

The 'having' orientation in the 21st century

We can find social critique closely resembling some of Fromm's ideas in James'[13] recent writings. James suggests that an increase in our economic well-being is not reflected in measures of psychological health such as levels of aggression, depression, addiction and relationship breakdown. He claims that 'advance capitalism makes money out of misery and dissatisfaction, as if it were encouraging us to fill the psychic void with material goods'.[14] Compare this comment to Fromm's assessment: 'Our attitude of consumption is symbolized by the open mouth. We fill ourselves up with all sorts of things without a really active effort, without genuine participation. We pay for being filled up.'[15] In his recent book *Affluenza*[16] James draws directly on Fromm's analysis of the insanity and vacuousness of consumerism.

Supermarkets, Fromm suggests, symbolize our obsession with 'having' in society. They give us a distorted notion of choice: 'We are not free to buy except what is on the shelves. We often buy what we don't really need and we often don't realize to what extent our "needs" and our "desires" have been programmed into us by advertising or what you might call brainwashing.'[17] Again, this certainly touches a chord in current debates about the power of supermarkets. It is also telling to observe that the slightly tongue-in-cheek expression of 'retail therapy' has become a shorthand way of describing how we try to comfort ourselves with new clothes or gadgets when things go wrong in our lives. Fromm's concerns are topical and important in bringing to our attention the dangers of the 'having' mode which leads us to rely on material goods for needs which should be addressed through human relating.

Fromm had very negative views of the media in his time and their role in keeping us anchored in empty 'having' orientations. He criticized their manipulative potential, and called for specific government intervention to end 'advertising of all harmful products... and ads with hidden emotional, irrational appeal. It would force advertisers to tell only facts.'[18] Some advertising (for example of tobacco) has been severely curtailed. However, advertising which plays on our identity needs (for example linking products to beauty, power and sexuality) remains dominant.

He singles out television as being particularly hypnotic in its seducing us to consume its messages eagerly and uncritically.[19] Time spent in front of the television screen is significant, with eight out of ten men and women in England reporting that watching television is their main leisure activity (ahead of spending time with family and friends).[20] The passivity of television watching has led to criticisms. Children grow up with images that almost become a reality for them – but one in which they are inert recipients rather than active creators.

The media also play a part in our celebrity culture. A false sense of relatedness is fostered as screen and magazine images invite us into the homes of our icons to find out details about their habits, tastes and life patterns. Further identification is sought as we buy not only their music or films but also the clothes or perfumes which bear their names. Fromm's summary of 'celebrity cult' in his time still seems entirely topical:

> In present-day Western society there is a peculiar interconnection between the narcissism of the celebrity and the needs of the public. The latter wants to be in touch with famous people because the life of the average person is empty and boring. The mass media live from selling fame, and thus everybody is satisfied; the narcissistic performer, the public, and the fame merchants.[21]

While this is a common assessment of what we perceive as the celebrity cult in our society, it is, however, worth maintaining some scepticism. Is this really a new development? After all, in previous centuries the 'celebrities' of the day – that is Royal courts – have also been trendsetters for lifestyle from fashion to food. Nonetheless, this is clearly an area in which we should maintain critical watchfulness in order to guard our sense of reality and identity.

'Having', 'doing' or 'being'?

Some social observers suggest that consumption is of key importance and has perhaps become the main way in which we define ourselves.[22] Accumulation of wealth seems to be a main aim in many people's lives, and people evaluate themselves and others by the price of their cars, houses, clothes and gadgets.

In addition, a further aspect of Fromm's analysis can be applied to developments in our own times. In our working lives 'busy-ness' seems to abound. Pressures at work with long working hours, increasing administrative duties and endless lists of emails are mirrored by the 'need' to be busy when we are not on duty. We 'have to' do the shopping, go to the gym, wash the car and keep up with the latest computer games as if to be seen to do nothing somehow undermines our importance.

Thus we can argue that in the early years of the 21st century a particular aspect of the 'having' orientation has become widespread. Increasingly, we appear to be caught up in a related style, namely in a *doing* mode in which incessant busy-ness has become a main defence against existential anxieties. In *To Have or To Be?* Fromm makes the useful distinction between two different types of activity: *productive activity* describes the positive way in which we can use our human powers. It originates from our own mental or emotional experience and is thus linked to the *being* mode.[23] Fromm contrasts this with *non-productive activity*, described as alienated, relentless busy-ness, driven either by external factors and incessant deadlines or else by internal compulsion.

Fromm highlights its relevance in modern capitalism:

> The concept of 'activity' rests upon one of the most widespread of man's illusions in modern industrial society. Our whole culture is geared to activity – activity in the sense of being busy … (the busyness necessary for business). In fact, most people are so 'active' that they cannot stand doing nothing; they even transform their so-called leisure time into another form of activity. If you are not active making money, you are active driving around, playing golf or just chatting about nothing. What is dreaded is the moment in which you have

really nothing 'to do'. ... They constantly need stimulus from the outside. ... And they imagine themselves to be immensely active while they are driven by the obsession to do something in order to escape the anxiety that is aroused when they are confronted with themselves.[24]

He suggests that 'busyness is the means to protect one from the torture of being in the land of the shadows'.[25]

To what extent is this now not just an issue for some individuals but also a concern on a societal level? More recent social observers point to a similar picture. Gergen[26] describes a multiphrenic, saturated self in the face of an ever increasing range of information and stimulation. Also, we are lured into spending more and more time on the process of 'having'. Shopping as a pastime and holiday activity is promoted in ever new and different ways. In the name of 'choice' we are encouraged to compare prices of goods and services. We may make savings but the 'activity' of finding out how to save money costs us time, not to mention energy. For those already struggling to make ends meet both financially and in terms of time and energy, this 'choice' adds further pressures. Schwartz adds further ideas on the 'paradox of choice': an obsession with choice in society means that we end up becoming passive and lose a sense of perspective.[27]

Reflection on how much time we spend in each activity mode – both in work and leisure time – could be interesting. Fortunately, discussions around life/work balance have increased in recent years, recognizing the importance of 'being' time in our lives where we experience ourselves as the originator of our actions in a positive way rather than being driven by ever increasing pressures.

These concerns do not only relate to busy adult working lives. With increasing pressures on children to 'perform' well at school and then gain precious university places, many young people can be seen to follow a timetable of relentless activities. This is not to suggest that 'doing nothing' should be the answer, and there are also current concerns about young people who have 'nothing to do'. After all, as Fromm suggests, productive activity can actually prevent destructiveness. Both these groups suffer from the common factor of not using their powers and energies most constructively: one group is driven by external pressures, the other by a lack of internal direction. We can see the usefulness of Fromm's 'being' concept here as a springboard for further investigation and initiatives, and as a stimulus to developing new and more fulfilling ways of living.

Social character and identity

Fromm's notion of a 'social character' provides a way in which individuals and societies can be analysed in terms of their predominant mode of relating to the world and to others. Funk follows up Fromm's thread in highlighting how people have come to define themselves through their acquisitions and are overly dependent on technology. For example, we can feel utterly lost when our mobile phones are stolen or when our computer networks break down, and we don't know what to do with ourselves when entertainment is not provided for us from external sources.[28] Such analyses are useful in highlighting weaknesses and gaps in society. However, we need to be careful not to use these terms to stereotype others simply because their behaviour appears to fit the scheme on a superficial level.

National identities pose a particular challenge according to Fromm. While he regarded a measured sense of concern for the well-being of communities as useful, he saw over-identification with one's nation as a sign that we have not quite moved forward to fully developed freedom and are hanging onto old connections to blood and soil (see Chapter 5). His call was for more individuation on the one hand but he felt that this had to be accompanied by a sense of global solidarity.

What are we to make of national identity in contemporary society? Pressures of globalization and personal choices have led to migration across borders and continents. Concerns are raised that national identities might be eroded. Countries struggle to define 'their' identities in the context of cultural and religious diversity and fear the loss of the symbols (from money to language) which characterize old certainties.

An interesting link to Fromm's ideas emerges in recent research into European identity. Although not referring directly to Fromm, some of the topics which Robyn[29] discusses reflect distinct echoes of his thinking. For example, he raises concerns over increasing nationalism and refers to 'almost existential questions'[30] arising from people trying to make sense of social changes such as German reunification and wider European developments. Fromm's focus on identity and the options he outlines for resolution of this issue are clearly relevant. As nations perceive threats to their identities, a turn to regressive isolationism may result. The rational alternative would be to progress onto heightened awareness of the commonality of humanistic principles which go beyond nations. After all, no individual country can lay exclusive claim to values like solidarity, freedom, love, justice and tolerance. However, nationally elected politicians may not see Fromm's cherished idea of global humanism as a priority.

Personal relationships in contemporary society

Fromm saw loving relatedness as the answer to our existential isolation. Further research has certainly confirmed its importance in personal relationships. The buffer effect of social support against various stressful life situations is well documented. It is good for our mental and physical health to have and to be loving partners and caring friends.[31] In the interpersonal sphere, Fromm's call for love, based on the attitudes of care, responsibility, respect and knowledge, is thus clearly still an important message.

Concerns have been raised over how modern technology has affected our interpersonal relating. Clark directly refers to Fromm in his discussion of the finding that Britons spend more time on social networking sites than do citizens of other European countries. Clark suggests that obsession with technology and 'collecting' friends in cyberspace undermines opportunities for real relating and building social support networks. Clark's strong message is reminiscent of Fromm's forcefulness: 'We live in a society where hardly anyone trusts anyone else, one in which narcissism and the cult of self, instead of being decried, is positively encouraged, by television, the media and by the big corporations who benefit from it.'[32] As with some of Fromm's exaggerated claims we can question Clark's assertion that 'hardly anyone trusts anyone else'. Friendship, respect and care are hopefully more common than suggested here. However, the concern expressed is indeed important.

On the other hand, perhaps social networking sites should not be the only focus of our disquiet over technology in society. After all, some of these sites allow us to keep in touch with geographically distant but emotionally close friends much as in the past the first telephone lines would have made such connections easier. A more worrying development might be the erosion of opportunities for forging looser support networks precipitated by the demise of post offices, local banks and small stores. While technology in internet banking and shopping may appear to make life more convenient for customers (and cuts costs for the operators) the closure of shops and banks contributes to the loss of a sense of community in towns and villages and reduces opportunities for real human relating.

Professional relationships in contemporary society

What can we take forward from Fromm's approach to therapy into aspects of working with people in counselling, social work, health or educational contexts in the 21st century? As we saw in Chapter 4, trying to outline a Frommian approach to therapy runs the risk of becoming a fragmented exercise with rather less pieces than necessary to make up a whole picture. His way of therapeutic relating generally comes across as a selection of psychoanalytic elements applied from a humanistic standpoint, along with judicious use of direct interventions.

Psychotherapy and counselling

Several decades on from his own practice, some of these ideas have indeed been taken forward. Qualities like the therapist's genuine interest and regard for the patient as well as the use of skills to challenge clients' views of themselves are spelled out in a number of approaches in health professional and social work training.[33] Techniques facilitating clients' abilities to express themselves through story telling echo Fromm's use of intuition and imagination in therapy. The importance of supervision and encouragement of a self-reflective approach in professional relating have become much more widely recognized in a number of areas such as nursing, teaching and youth work. This is not to say that Fromm's work necessarily influenced these developments. After all, he was not the first person to express these ideas, nor will he be the last. The importance of his contribution lies in the fact that he spelled out so clearly and strongly the message of commitment to reflection, growth and love and examined its significance in therapeutic interventions in the modern world.

The prominence which Fromm gives to the quality of professional relationships gains support from recent research. For example, studies into the resilience of children and young people in difficult circumstances firmly point to the value of genuine relating with adults, whether professionals, family members or volunteers.[34] This is a particularly challenging idea in today's society of intensely monitored accountability and target driven approaches. The very qualities which Fromm highlights – intuition and creativity – appear to jar with such prescriptions.

Furthermore, concerns about risk assessment and the concomitant need for extensive, at times perhaps excessive, bureaucracy and administration may also undermine productive relating and could actually prevent suitable adults from coming forward, for example as volunteers in community groups. This is of course not to deny the need for realistic risk assessments but Fromm's ideas help to remind us that human relating should be at the centre of our therapeutic interventions.

Thus Fromm provides food for thought not just at the level of one-to-one relating with patients or clients but at a wider institutional level, too. To what extent have administrative burdens and a focus on results rather than processes become barriers to professionals expressing genuine interest in people? In what ways have our fears about boundaries limited the depth of relating which can be achieved in professional relationships? This may be a wake-up call for institutions to re-examine their structures in terms of how they affect their frontline workers' potential for creative relating.

Education in contemporary society

In education, too, Fromm emphasizes the need for a focus on the quality of interactions within a social context. We can argue that since Fromm's days, there have been more initiatives to take account of pupils in a holistic way. Schools have introduced lessons in citizenship and social education, and Fromm might agree with the potential they offer. Wehr[35] suggests that some of Fromm's concepts of biophilia and productive relating between pupils and teachers provide a useful basis for education in contemporary society. This includes teachers approaching pupils with genuine interest and a balance of loving acceptance and discipline.

However, the following statement also seems to apply: 'Not only industrial production is ruled by the principle of continuous and limitless acceleration. The educational system has the same criterion: the more college graduates, the better. ... Few people raise the question of *quality* or what all this increase in quantity is good for.'[36]

Quality issues have indeed been raised – but on occasions only in the sense of quantification and competition. League tables put pressures on teachers and students to jump through examination hoops, at times losing sight of creativity and learning. Fromm sees education as a much broader process, not separate from what goes on in wider society: 'I believe that education means to acquaint the young with the best heritage of the human race ... it is effective only if ... words become reality in the person of the teacher and in the practice and structure of society.'[37] Fromm also reminds us that this needs to be a society-wide process. While teachers can endeavour to develop a humanistically orientated approach towards their pupils, this will only succeed if they are supported in this work by corresponding values and practice in society more generally.

Fromm also questions the rigidity of the age brackets in primary and secondary education, suggesting that many people would learn much better in their thirties and forties when they are more mature and may feel the need to change the occupation they chose in their youth. He proposes that we should be completely free to do so,[38] and he would be pleased to note the changing demographic picture of people in education in the UK since the 1960s, heralded by the Open University.

Work in contemporary society

As we have seen, work was an issue of particular concern for Fromm in that it can be linked to a number of his existential issues. The relatedness and sense of identity which work can bring have frequently been highlighted. However, in the workplace within Western capitalism, our needs for relatedness are not necessarily met. James draws attention to the negative effects of an 'increase in competitiveness and assessment in the work-place'[39] in conditions which encourage social comparison and excessive self-centredness. Fromm suggests that by putting economics at the forefront, the human agenda is pushed into the background and a sense of hostility or lack of concern can result.[40]

Fromm's view of *humanistic management* highlights the importance of workplace relating. According to his vision, alienated bureaucratic relating should be replaced by a system in which workers are given the opportunity to be part of the process of the decision making, to feel heard and valued. Such a system would address their needs for relatedness and a sense of identity. Arguably, human relating along these lines already happens in many organizations. However, the need for the application of Fromm's ideas is perhaps especially important for large multi- and transnational companies in which workers and to some extent managers are cut adrift from any conceptualization of their product in relation to human needs.

In the current climate of rising unemployment it is also essential that we acknowledge the human costs associated with this. If work no longer provides a source of identity and opportunities for relationship building, how else can these needs be addressed? Taking Fromm's ideas on board we would be well advised to pay particular attention to the way in which education and voluntary work can help individuals to find meaning while they are not in paid employment. Governments should encourage such schemes (in conjunction with a concern for the financial impact of unemployment) to support the mental health of their citizens.

Community relations in contemporary society

The extent to which the development of productive relating is facilitated or hindered by current community practices is clearly a complex area, widely discussed by social observers on both sides of the Atlantic.

The more recent notion of social capital has addressed some of the issues of relatedness which Fromm raises. This term has been defined as 'features of social life – networks, norms and trust – that enable participants to act together more effectively to pursue shared objectives'.[41] Concerns over the loss of relating through 'community spirit' have been voiced in the USA with the suggestion that: 'most Americans today feel vaguely and uncomfortably disconnected'.[42]

Putnam provides an incisive account of the development of civic disengagement in US communities, charting the decline of community organizations. Based on his detailed social analysis he highlights the need for renewed civic engagement and building of social capital as an individual *and* a social issue, to be addressed at all levels of human interaction, from extracurricular activities for young people to bringing people back to the ballot box. We could imagine Fromm agreeing with some of these measures. A further parallel emerges from Putnam's view that television is at least in part to blame for people having less time to spend on community activities. As we have seen, Fromm had a critical view of the media and feared that technology could undermine human relating, evidenced also in his research with Mexican farming communities, where the arrival of cinema and radio heralded an end to numerous shared cultural activities.[43]

However, we may also want to turn some of these issues on their head. Putnam notes the trends toward civic disengagement from the 1960s onwards. Might writers like Fromm proclaiming on the importance of individuality actually have contributed to this decline? After all, a call like Fromm's to avoid 'herd conformity' would be unlikely to make us rush to join established clubs. This again points to the difficulties in balancing relatedness and individuality needs against one another and suggests that our attempts to maintain an equilibrium will continue to require further thought and action.

Political concerns in contemporary society

Fromm also took a pessimistic view of the way in which politicians present themselves and he questions whether they really follow a democratic agenda. In a system which does not specifically address human values, the political leadership reflects this, too: 'the selfishness the system generates makes leaders value personal success more highly than social responsibility'.[44] As he suggests, politicians should aim for honesty and transparency as opposed to self-centred electioneering. Equally, voters need to re-examine their motivations and lose their blinkered focus on 'what's in it for me?'.

Furthermore Fromm suggests that the machinery of political parties has alienated the voter:

the methods of political propaganda tend to increase the feeling of insignificance of the individual voter. Repetition of slogans and emphasis on factors which have nothing to do with the issue at stake numb his critical capacities. The clear and rational appeal to his thinking are rather the exception than the rule in political propaganda – even in democratic countries ... the individual voter cannot help feeling small and of little significance.[45]

Fromm's remedy for this is a participatory democracy in which voters have the opportunity to be involved in decision making processes more directly. Wilde suggests that 'Fromm's work resolutely opposes the creeping fatalism of contemporary social and political life'.[46] While some measures in tune with Fromm's ideas – for example focus groups organized by health trusts – are now being introduced, further discussions are clearly necessary.

Ecological concerns in contemporary society

A critical area which shows Fromm as prescient is our contradictory relationship with nature – being part of it on the one hand but on the other trying to control, conquer and exploit it. His claim that 'industrial society has contempt for nature'[47] is now almost taken for granted, as further news of our role in the development of climate change stares at us from almost daily media headlines. His question: *'Is There an Alternative to Catastrophe?'*[48] would not seem amiss now in a context of increasing knowledge and worry about our influence on our natural environment. While Fromm's main concern was the threat of a global nuclear war, the dangers of greenhouse gases have become a particularly dark cloud looming on our horizon. Climate change has virtually become an accepted reality as the vast majority of experts no longer regard it as a hypothesis whose validity is yet to be established. Indeed, a film about its consequences, *An Inconvenient Truth*, brought its creator Al Gore a Nobel Prize for Peace in 2007. The details of global threats may have shifted but Fromm's claim that 'for the first time in history the *physical survival of the human race depends on a radical change of the human heart'*[49] sounds entirely up to date.

In 1991 Ingleby pointed to the continued – and even increasing – relevance of Fromm's ideas. We could argue that almost twenty years later we need to revisit Fromm's views with further urgency due to growing threats (or at least heightened awareness of them) from accelerating climate change and global terrorism. While in Fromm's time consumerism was seen mainly as an individual and social issue, it has now also become a global concern as excessive 'having' orientations are threatening the survival of our planet as we know it.

Taking Fromm's ideas forward

As the above exploration suggests, the time is ripe for another look at Fromm's ideas. His emphasis on an ethical approach at a number of levels in everyday life, political institutions and 'One World' politics[50] are perhaps now needed more than ever. His thoughts can be seen as a powerful message for our time. In order to develop a society and relationships in tune with our human needs, we have to approach life with a basic stance of respect and mindfulness both towards ourselves and those to whom we relate in daily life. Further, such an orientation is also essential as a basis from which international political and economic connections are forged.

What makes Fromm's analysis particularly meaningful is his framework of existential issues as a starting point. His emphasis on our need for relatedness, and associated with this, for transcendence, rootedness, identity and a system of values, provides potent food for thought. Unlike many other social critics, he includes in his theory psychological needs which may explain individual actions and give a basis for a positive way forward on a personal level. Unlike many therapists and counsellors, however, he emphasizes the importance of working on social structures which make sane living possible. In this way neither individual nor social institutions are let off the hook: we cannot take our eyes off either our own personal development and relationships *or* the wider social agenda. Any plans for improving our mental health must operate on both levels: a common sense approach yet a surprisingly uncommonly discussed one, too. It is this dialectic which makes Fromm's focus on love and respect unique, and it is certainly worth reminding ourselves of his ideas.

While we could argue that Fromm's attempt to trace humanism across different thought and belief systems may reduce them to their lowest common denominator, perhaps this is the only denominator which we currently have available to provide a basis for sane living. Fromm's position may be a wise one to adopt on pragmatic grounds. A focus on commonality and basic agreement between different belief systems could be beneficial in fostering a sense of unity and harmony between communities. Furthermore, in linking each of the main world religions to humanistic values, Fromm also offers their followers a way of reconciling their beliefs with social systems which are based on humanistic principles. Provided societies follow this common core of values, the faithful need not see their beliefs as at odds with the social order. An emphasis on shared ideals allows for a vision of how their convictions can be lived out in societies in which humanistic values are embedded.

The comprehensiveness of Fromm's message of love arising from our existential needs for individuals and societies would seem to offer new yet old ways of approaching developments in our time. These are difficult issues and there are no easy answers. Fromm's views are unlikely to set tomorrow's political and moral agenda all on their own. However, they can contribute to an impetus to look at ourselves and society in helpful ways. As he himself suggested:

> there are no prescriptions for loving life, but much can be learned. If you can shed illusions, seeing others and yourself as they are and you are, if you can learn how to be still rather than always 'going places', if you can grasp the distinction between life and things, between happiness and thrill, between means and ends, and – most of all – between love and force, you will have made the first step towards loving life.[51]

References and Notes

Chapter 1

1 Most of the biographical information used in this chapter comes from two sources:

R. Funk (2000) *Erich Fromm. His Life and Ideas. An Illustrated Biography*, New York: Continuum International Publishing.

R. Funk (2001) *Erich Fromm. Mit Selbstzeugnissen und Bilddokumenten*, Rororo Bildmonographie 322, 8. Auflage, Reinbek: Rowohlt Taschenbuch Verlag.

To avoid cluttering the text too much with notes and references I will not cite these two books each time I draw on them (other than for direct quotations). Any other sources will be clearly identified in the endnotes.

Fromm's collected works will be referred to frequently throughout this book. Full details will be given on the first occasion in each chapter; thereafter the abbreviation 'GA' for 'Gesamtausgabe' will be used. Where relevant I will indicate in brackets the original publication date and title. Any translations from this back into English are mine.

2 L. Friedman (2006) 'Recovering Erich Fromm's Life: Some Dilemmas and Preliminary Solutions', *Fromm Forum* 10/2006, Tübingen: International Erich Fromm Society, p. 13.

3 E. Fromm (1999) *Erich Fromm Gesamtausgabe in zwölf Bänden* (ed. R. Funk) *Band XI Politische Psychoanalyse, Schriften aus dem Nachlass*, Stuttgart: Deutsche Verlags-Anstalt, p. 617 (1974 'Im Namen des Lebens', radio interview with Hans Jürgen Schultz).

4 R. Funk (2000) *op. cit.*, p. 21.

5 L. Friedman (2006) *op. cit.*, p. 15.

6 R. Funk (2000) *op. cit.*, p. 20.

7 E. Fromm, 1977 TV interview, cited in R. Funk (2000) *op. cit.*, p. 10.

8 R. I. Evans (1981) *Dialogue with Erich Fromm*, New York: Praeger Publishers, p. 57 (originally published in 1966, New York: Harper & Row).

9 E. Fromm (1999) *op. cit.*, p. 618.

10 Cited in R. Funk (2000) *op. cit.*, p. 37.

11 E. Fromm (1999) *Erich Fromm GA VI Religion*, pp. 80–81 (1975 'Die Aktualität der prophetischen Schriften' – radio talk).

12 Cited in R. Funk (2000) *op. cit.*, p. 54.

13 *Ibid.*, p. 55.

14 Freud's basic assumptions are introduced and discussed in another volume of the 'Mindshapers' series: R. Stevens (2008) *Sigmund Freud: Examining the Essence of his Contribution*, Basingstoke: Palgrave Macmillan.

15 E. Fromm (1980) *Arbeiter und Angestellte am Vorabend des Dritten Reiches. Eine sozialpsychologische Untersuchung*, bearbeitet und herausgegeben von Wolfgang Bonss, Stuttgart: Deutsche Verlags-Anstalt (original publication: *German Workers 1929 – A Survey, its Methods and Results*).
16 R. Funk (2000) *op. cit.*, p. 98, cited from a memorandum which Fromm wrote to a lawyer regarding the termination of his contract.
17 R. Funk (2000) *op. cit.*, p. 99, cited from a letter from Horkheimer to Leo Löwenthal on 31/10/1942.
18 E. Fromm (1999) *GA XII Psychoanalyse und Kunst des Lebens, Schriften aus dem Nachlass* (1969 'Infantilization and Dispair Maskerading as Radicalism', German version translated by R. Funk), pp. 97–111.
19 D. Burston (1991) *The Legacy of Erich Fromm*, Cambridge (Mass.) and London: Harvard University Press, pp. 226–227.
20 E. Fromm (1980) *op. cit.*
21 The change of title between the USA and UK publications is interesting to note: the US title, which includes *Escape* seems to carry more active connotations while the word *Fear* in the UK title suggests a more guarded and passive approach.
22 E. Fromm (2001) *The Fear of Freedom*, Abingdon: Routledge Classics, p. 90.
23 This group included for example Clara Thompson, Edward S. Tauber, Rose Spiegel and David E. Schecter whose accounts of supervision experiences with Fromm are mentioned in Chapter 4 of this book.
24 R. I. Evans (1981) *op. cit.*, p. 121.
25 R. Funk (1994) 'Foreword' (trans. L. W. Garmer), in: E. Fromm (1994) *The Art of Listening*, London: Constable, p. 8.
26 R. Funk (2001) *op. cit.*, p. 137, my translation.
27 E. Fromm (1999) *GA XI*, *op. cit.*, p. 629.
28 R. Funk (1982) *The Courage to Be Human* (trans. M. Shaw), New York: Continuum, p. xiv.
29 See for example D. Burston (1991) *op. cit.*

Chapter 2

1   E. Fromm (1979) *To Have or To Be?*, London: Abacus, p. 10.
2   *Ibid.*
3   E. Fromm (2002) *The Sane Society*, Abingdon: Routledge Classics, p. 345.
4   E. Fromm (2001) *op. cit.*, p. 17.
5   E. Fromm (2002) *op. cit.*, p. 26.
6   See H. J. Allen (1992) 'Fromm's Humanism and Rorty's Historicism', *Contemporary Psychoanalysis*, 28, pp. 467–482 (Fromm Archive).
7   E. Fromm (2002) *op. cit.*, p. 36.
8   E. Fromm (1997) *The Anatomy of Human Destructiveness*, London: Pimlico, p. 318.
9   E. Fromm (2002) *op. cit.*, p. 23.
10 E. Fromm (1968) *The Revolution of Hope. Towards a Humanized Technology*, New York: Harper & Row, p. 62.
11 For a summary and discussion of Erikson's ideas, see for example R. Stevens (2008) *Erik H. Erikson: Explorer of Identity and the Life-Cycle*, Basingstoke: Palgrave Macmillan.
12 E. Fromm (2002) *op. cit.*, p. 64.
13 E. Fromm (1968) *op. cit.*, p. 89.

14 E. Fromm (1980) *Beyond the Chains of Illusion. My Encounter with Marx and Freud*, London: Abacus, p. 166.

15 E. Fromm (2002) *op. cit.*, p. 268.

16 E. Fromm (1999) *Erich Fromm Gesamtausgabe in zwölf Bänden* (ed. R. Funk) *Band II Analytische Charaktertheorie*, Stuttgart: Deutscher Taschenbuch Verlag (1947 'Man for Himself. An enquiry into the Psychology of Ethics', German trans. P. Stapf and I. Mühsam), p. 44.

17 E. Fromm (1997) *op. cit.*, p. 439 ff.

18 E. Fromm (2002) *op. cit.*, pp. 33–34, see also R. Funk (1982) *The Courage to Be Human* (trans. M. Shaw), New York: Continuum, p. 43.

19 E. Fromm (1999) *GA II* (1964 'The Heart of Man', German trans. Liselotte and Ernst Mickel), p. 204.

20 M. Maccoby (2008) 'Fromm Didn't Want to Be a Frommian', in: R. Funk (2009) (ed.) *The Clinical Erich Fromm. Personal Accounts and Papers on Therapeutic Technique*, Amsterdam-New York: Rodopi.

21 D.E. Schecter (1981 and 1958) 'To Be Truly with Him One Felt Fully Alive and Awake', in: R. Funk (2009) *op. cit.*

22 E. Fromm (1999) *GA II*, p. 76.

23 E. Fromm (2002) *op. cit.*, p. 76.

24 E. Fromm (1999) *GA III Empirische Untersuchungen zum Gesellschafts-Charakter* (1970 'Social Character in a Mexican Village. A Sociopsychoanalytic Study', trans. Liselotte and Ernst Mickel), p. 233.

25 *Ibid.*, p. 399.

26 *Ibid.*, p. 411.

27 E. Fromm (2001) *op. cit.*, pp. 23–24.

28 *Ibid.*, p. 20.

29 R. M. Crowley (1981) 'He Was Dedicated to Mankind', in: R. Funk (2009) *op. cit.*, p. 101.

30 E. Fromm (2002) *op. cit.*, p. 67.

31 *Ibid.*

32 M. Maccoby (2008) *op. cit.*, pp. 53–54.

33 E. Fromm (2001) *op. cit.*, pp. 26–27.

34 E. Fromm (1968) *op. cit.*, p. 60.

35 E. Fromm (2001) *op. cit.*, p. 28.

36 *Ibid.*

37 *Ibid.*, p. 228.

38 E. Fromm (1980) *op. cit.*, p. 169.

39 E. Fromm (2001) *op. cit.*, p. 27.

40 See for example L. Wilde (2004) *Erich Fromm and the Quest for Solidarity*, Basingstoke: Palgrave Macmillan.

41 E. Fromm (1968) *op. cit.*, p. 66.

42 L. Wilde (2004) *op. cit.*

43 E. Fromm (2001) *op. cit.*, p. 30.

44 E. Fromm (1968) *op. cit.*, p. 67.

45 *Ibid.*, p. 89.

46 *Ibid.*, p. 67.

47 *Ibid.*

48 E. Fromm (1968) *op. cit.*, p. 17.

49 R. Frie (2003) 'Erich Fromm and Contemporary Psychoanalysis: From Modernism to Postmodernism', *The Psychoanalytic Review*, 90, 6, pp. 855–868 (Fromm Archive).

50 E. Fromm (1999) *GA II*, pp. 162–163.

51 *Ibid.*, p. 3.

52 D. Ingleby (1991) 'Introduction', in: E. Fromm (2002) *The Sane Society*, London: Routledge Classics, p. xvi.
53 E. Fromm (2001) *op. cit.*, p. 214.
54 R. Funk (2008) 'Direct Encounter with the Other', in: R. Funk (2009) *op. cit.*
55 Letter to Clara Urquhart 29/9/1962 (Fromm Archive).
56 E. Fromm (1980) *op. cit.*, p. 165.
57 *Ibid.*
58 E. S. Tauber (1979) 'Clinician and Social Philosopher', *Contemporary Psychoanalysis*, 15, 2, pp. 201–213 (Fromm Archive).
59 E. Fromm (1968) *op. cit.*, p. 91.
60 E. Fromm *GA II*, p. 76.
61 J. H. Schaar (1961) *Escape from Authority: The Perspectives of Erich Fromm*, New York: Basic Books, p. 109.
62 E. Fromm (1980) *op. cit.*, p. 171.
63 J. H. Schaar (1961) *op. cit.*, p. 7.

Chapter 3

1   R. Funk (2008) '"Direct" Encounter with the Other', in: R. Funk (2009) (ed.) *The Clinical Erich Fromm. Personal Accounts and Papers on Therapeutic Technique*, Amsterdam-New York: Rodopi.
2   R. Spiegel (1980) 'A Touching of the Selves of Two Persons', in: R. Funk (2009) *op. cit.*
3   See for example J. Silva Garcia (1989) 'Erich Fromm in Mexico: 1950–1973', *Contemporary Psychoanalysis*, pp. 244–257 (Fromm Archive).
4   R. Funk (2006) 'Liebe im Leben von Erich Fromm', *Fromm Forum* 11/2006, Tübingen: International Erich Fromm Society, p. 16.
5   R. Funk, personal communication, July 2006.
6   R. Funk (2008) *op. cit.*
7   E. Fromm (1975) *The Art of Loving*, London: Unwin Paperbacks, p. 15.
8   *Ibid.*
9   *Ibid.*, p. 22.
10 E. Fromm (2002) *op. cit.*, p. 30.
11 E. Fromm (1975) *op. cit.*, p. 27.
12 *Ibid.*, p. 28.
13 *Ibid.*, p. 29.
14 *Ibid.*, p. 51.
15 *Ibid.*, p. 90.
16 *Ibid.*, p. 93.
17 *Ibid.*
18 *Ibid.*
19 E. Fromm (1999) *Erich Fromm Gesamtausgabe in zwölf Bänden* (ed. R. Funk) *Band II Analytische Charaktertheorie*, Stuttgart: Deutscher Taschenbuch Verlag, p. 102 (1947 'Man for Himself. An Enquiry into the Psychology of Ethics', German version trans. P. Stapf and I. Mühsam).
20 M. Maccoby (2008) 'Fromm Didn't Want to Be a Frommian', in: R. Funk (2009) (ed.) *The Clinical Erich Fromm. Personal Accounts and Papers on Therapeutic Technique*, Amsterdam-New York: Rodopi.
21 E. Fromm (1975) *op. cit.*, p. 97.
22 *Ibid.*, p. 94.

23 *Ibid.*, p. 95.
24 *Ibid.*, p. 98.
25 *Ibid.*, p. 100.
26 *Ibid.*
27 *Ibid.*, p. 44.
28 E. Fromm (2001) *The Fear of Freedom*, Abingdon: Routledge Classics, p. 99.
29 E. Fromm (1975) *op. cit.*, p. 100.
30 *Ibid.*, p. 102.
31 E. S. Tauber (1980) 'A Man Whose Words are Ways', in: R. Funk (2009) *op. cit.*
32 E. Fromm (1975) *op. cit.*, p. 106.
33 *Ibid.*, p. 109.
34 *Ibid.*, p. 45.
35 H. J. Schultz (2000) 'Erich Fromm: Humanist ohne Illusion – Eine Hommage', *Fromm Forum* 4/2000, Tübingen: International Erich Fromm Society.
36 See for example J. Oates, C. Lewis and M. E. Lamb (2005) 'Parenting and Attachment', in: S. Ding and K. Littleton (eds) *Children's Personal and Social Development*, Oxford: Blackwell.
37 E. Fromm (1975) *op. cit.*, p. 49.
38 *Ibid.*, p. 50.
39 *Ibid.*, p. 49.
40 *Ibid.*, p. 51.
41 E. Fromm (1997) *The Anatomy of Human Destructiveness*, London: Pimlico, p. 125.
42 E. Fromm (1975) *op. cit.*, p. 35.
43 E. Fromm (1999) *GA IX Sozialistischer Humanismus und humanistische Ethik* (1972 'Der Traum ist die Sprache des universalen Menschen' – Radio talk).
44 See for example R. Stevens (2008) *Freud: Shaper of the Unconscious Mind*, Basingstoke: Palgrave Macmillan.
45 E. Fromm (1975) *op. cit.*, p. 34.
46 *Ibid.*, pp. 33–34.
47 *Ibid.*, p. 34.
48 E. Fromm (1999) *GA XII Psychoanalyse und Kunst des Lebens, Schriften aus dem Nachlass, Register der Bände XI und XII* (1940 'Changing Concepts of Homo-sexuality in Psychoanalysis', German trans. R. Funk).
49 E. Fromm (1999) *GA XII op. cit.*, pp. 537–538.
50 E. Fromm (2001) *op. cit.*, p. 100.
51 E. Fromm (1975) *op. cit.*, p. 56.
52 *Ibid.*, p. 18.
53 E. Fromm (1979) *To Have or To Be?*, London: Abacus, p. 118.
54 See for example C. Leadbeater (1999) *Living on Thin Air: The New Economy*, London: Viking.
55 E. Fromm (1975) *op. cit.*, p. 22.
56 *Ibid.*, pp. 75–76.
57 *Ibid.*, p. 76.
58 *Ibid.*, p. 25.
59 See for example S. Duck (1999) 'Developing a Steady and Exclusive Partnership', in: S. Duck (ed.) *Relating to Others*, Second Edition, Buckingham: Open University Press.
60 E. Fromm (1975) *op. cit.*, p. 87.
61 *Ibid.*, p. 52.
62 *Ibid.*, p. 76.
63 E. Fromm (1994) *The Art of Listening*, London: Constable, p. 84.
64 *Ibid.*, p. 83.

65   For example C. Rini, K. DuHamel, J. Ostroff, F. Boulad, R. Martini, L. Mee, S. Sexon, S. Manne, J. Austin, S. K. Parsons, S. E. Williams and W. H. Redd (2008) 'Social Support from Family and Friends as a Buffer of Low Spousal Support among Mothers of Critically Ill Children: A Multilevel Modelling Approach', *Health Psychology*, 27, 5, pp. 593–603.

66   See for example M. Argyle (2001) *The Psychology of Happiness*, Second Edition, Hove: Routledge.

67   D. Burston (1991) *The Legacy of Erich Fromm*, Cambridge (Mass.) and London: Harvard University Press, p. 22.

68   See for example Christopher Badock (2000) *Evolutionary Psychology: A Critical Introduction*, Cambridge: Polity Press.

69   See for example D. M. Buss (1998) 'The Psychology of Human Mate Selection: Exploring the Complexity of the Strategic Repertoire', in: C. Crawford and D. L. Krebs (eds) (1998) *Handbook of Evolutionary Psychology: Ideas, Issues and Applications*, London: Lawrence Erlbaum Associates.

70   E. Fromm (1999) *GA VIII Psychoanalyse* (1943 'Sex and Character', German trans. C. Dietlmaier), p. 375.

71   L. Wilde (2004) 'The Significance of Maternalism in the Evolution of Fromm's Social Thought', *The European Legacy*, 9, 3, p. 352.

72   Recent work in the area of neurobiology could offer interesting new insights in relation to Fromm's ideas. For example, Zeki's studies in this area provides information on how brain processes appear to support bonding and attachment (see for example S. Zeki (2009) *Splendours and Miseries of the Brain. Love, Creativity and the Quest for Human Happiness*, Chichester: Wiley-Blackwell).

73   E. Fromm (1975) *op. cit.*, p. 50.

74   J. H Schaar (1961) *Escape from Authority: The Perspectives of Erich Fromm*, New York: Basic Books, p. 136.

75   H. Jellouschek (2006) 'Die Kunst des Liebens aus der Sicht eines Paartherapeuten', *Fromm Forum* 11/2006, Tübingen: Internationale Erich Fromm Gesellschaft, pp. 6–11.

76   *Ibid.*, p. 97.

77   *Ibid.*, p. 108.

78   E. Fromm (1975) *op. cit.*, p. 106.

79   E. Fromm (1975) *op. cit.*, p. 109.

Chapter 4

1   R. M. Lesser (1992) 'Frommian Therapeutic Practice: "A Few Rich Hours"', *Contemporary Psychoanalysis*, Vol. 28, pp. 483–494 (Fromm Archive).

2   G. Chrzanowski (1997) 'Erich Fromm's Escape from Sigmund Freud: An Introduction to "Escape from Freedom"', *International Forum of Psychoanalysis*, 6, 3, pp. 185–189 (Fromm Archive).

3   R. Funk (1994) 'Foreword', in: E. Fromm (1994) *The Art of Listening*, London: Constable, p. 11.

4   E. Fromm (1994) *The Art of Listening*, London: Constable, p. 192.

5   R. Funk (1994) *op. cit.*, p. 9.

6   R. Spiegel (1994) 'Reflections on Our Heritage from Erich Fromm. The Humanistic Ethics of Erich Fromm', *Contemporary Psychoanalysis*, Vol. 30, pp. 419–424 (Fromm Archive).

7   E. Fromm (1994) *op. cit.*, p. 98.
8   *Ibid.*, p. 45.
9   R. U. Akeret (1995) *Tales from a Traveling Couch. A Psychotherapist Revisits His Most Memorable Patients*, New York and London: Norton, pp. 112–124 (Fromm Archive).
10 S. Gojman de Millán (1996) 'The Analyst as a Person: Fromm's Approach to Psychoanalytic Theory and Practice', in: M. Cortina and M. Maccoby (eds) *A Prophetic Analyst. Erich Fromm's Contribution to Psychoanalysis*, Jason Aronson: Nothvale and London, pp. 235–258 (Fromm Archive).
11 R. U. Akeret (1995) *op. cit.*, pp. 112–124.
12 G. Chrzanowski (1998) *op. cit.*, p. 2.
13 E. Fromm (1994) *op. cit.*, p. 103.
14 *Ibid.*, p. 100.
15 E. Fromm (1999) *Erich Fromm Gesamtausgabe in zwölf Bänden* (ed. R. Funk) *Band XII Psychoanalyse und Kunst des Lebens, Schriften aus dem Nachlass, Register der Bände XI und XII*, Stuttgart: Deutsche Verlags-Anstalt (1955 'Remarks on The Problem of Free Association'), p. 200.
16 R. Funk (2000) *Erich Fromm. His Life and Ideas. An Illustrated Biography*, New York: Continuum International Publishing, p. 107.
17 B. Landis (1981a) 'Fromm's Approach to Psychoanalytic Technique', *Contemporary Psychoanalysis*, Vol. 17, 4, pp. 537–551 (Fromm Archive).
18 E. Fromm (1994) *op. cit.*, p. 90.
19 *Ibid.*, pp. 98–99.
20 See for example C. Rogers (1965) *Client-Centered Therapy*, Boston: Houghton Mifflin Company.
21 E. Fromm (1994) *op. cit.*, p. 29.
22 E. Fromm (1980b) *Greatness and Limitations of Freud's Thought*, London: Jonathan Cape, p. 39.
23 M. Horney Eckhardt (1990/2008) 'The Shift from Couch to Chair', in: R. Funk (2009) (ed.) *The Clinical Erich Fromm. Personal Accounts and Papers on Therapeutic Technique*, Amsterdam-New York: Rodopi.
24 B. Landis (1981a) *op. cit.*, pp. 537–551.
25 R. Funk (2008) 'Direct Encounter with the Other', in: R. Funk (2009) *op. cit.*
26 G. Khoury (2006) 'A Crucial Encounter: Erich Fromm', *Fromm Forum* 10/2006, Tübingen: International Erich Fromm Society, p. 20.
27 M. Horney Eckhardt (1990/2008) *op. cit.*, p. 34.
28 E. Fromm (1994) *op. cit.*, p. 121.
29 E. Fromm (1999) *GA IX Sozialistischer Humanismus und humanistische Ethik* (1951 'The Forgotten Language. An Introduction to the Understanding of Dreams, Fairy Tales and Myths', German trans. Liselotte and Ernst Mickel), p. 171.
30 E. Fromm (1994) *op. cit.*, p. 136.
31 *Ibid.*, p. 99.
32 E. Fromm (1980b) *op. cit.*, p. 72.
33 *Ibid.*, p. 101.
34 R. M. Lesser (1992) *op. cit.*, pp. 483–494.
35 R. U. Akeret (1975) 'Reminiscences of Supervision with Erich Fromm', *Contemporary Psychoanalysis*, Vol. 11, pp. 461–463.
36 E. Fromm (1994) *op. cit.*, p. 137.
37 E. Fromm (1999) *GA XII* (1955 'Remarks on The Problem of Free Association', German trans. R. Funk), p. 198.
38 E. Fromm (1994) *op. cit.*, p. 137.

39 See for example R. Stevens (2008) *Freud: Shaper of the Unconscious Mind*, Basing-stoke: Palgrave Macmillan.
40 E. Fromm (1994) *op. cit.*, p. 39.
41 B. Landis (1981b) 'Erich Fromm – The Conduct of Psychoanalysis' (Fromm Archive).
42 E. Fromm (1994) *op. cit.*, p. 29.
43 R. U. Akeret (1975) 'Reminiscences of Supervision with Erich Fromm', *Contemporary Psychoanalysis*, Vol. 11, pp. 461–463.
44 E. Fromm (1994) *op. cit.*, p. 50.
45 *Ibid.*, p. 41.
46 *Ibid.*, p. 75.
47 *Ibid.*, p. 41.
48 *Ibid.*, p. 40.
49 D. H. Ortmeyer (2008) 'A Remarkably Inquiring Mind', in: R. Funk (2009) *op. cit.*
50 E. Fromm (1994) *op. cit.*, p. 66.
51 E. Fromm (1999) *GA VIII Psychoanalyse* (1966 'The Oedipus Complex: Comments on "The Case of Little Hans"', German trans. Liselotte and Ernst Mickel), p. 147.
52 E. Fromm (1994) *op. cit.*, p. 53.
53 *Ibid.*, p. 55.
54 E. Fromm (1999) *GA XII* (1969 'The Dialectic Revision of Psychoanalysis', German trans. R. Funk), p. 58.
55 E. Fromm (1994) *op. cit.*, p. 53.
56 *Ibid.*, p. 26.
57 *Ibid.*, p. 27.
58 R. Funk (1994) 'Foreword', in: E. Fromm (1994) *op. cit.*, p. 7.
59 G. Chrzanowski (1998) *op. cit.*
60 R. M. Lesser (1992) *op. cit.*
61 E. S. Tauber (1981) 'Tributes', *Contemporary Psychoanalysis*, Vol. 17, No. 4, pp. 448–449 (Fromm Archive).
62 D. Burston (1991) *The Legacy of Erich Fromm*, Cambridge (Mass.) and London: Harvard University Press, p. 232.
63 R. Stevens (2008) *op. cit.*, p. 137.
64 E. Fromm (1994) *op. cit.*, p. 40.
65 *Ibid.*, p. 193.
66 E. Fromm (1975) *The Art of Loving*, London: Unwin Paperbacks, p. 28.
67 E. Fromm (1994) *op. cit.*, p. 53.
68 See for example N. Frude (2003) 'The Family: A Psychological Perspective', in: D. Watkins, J. Edwards and P. Gastrell (eds) *Community Health Nursing: Frameworks for Practice*, Second Edition, Edinburgh: Ballière Tindall.
69 S. Buechler (2006) 'Why We Need Fromm Today: Fromm's Work Ethic', *Fromm Forum* 10/2006, Tübingen: International Erich Fromm Society, p. 34.

Chapter 5

1 R. Funk, (2000) *Erich Fromm. His Life and Ideas. An Illustrated Biography*, New York: Continuum International Publishing, p. 164.
2 E. Fromm (2002) *The Sane Society*, Abingdon: Routledge Classics, p. 28.
3 *Ibid.*, p. 31.
4 E. Fromm (2001) *op cit.*, p. 122.
5 E. Fromm (2002) *op. cit.*, p. 36.

6   *Ibid.*, p. 44.
7   *Ibid.*, p. 57.
8   E. Fromm (1997) *The Anatomy of Human Destructiveness*, London: Pimlico, p. 276.
9   E. Fromm (2002) *op. cit.*, p. 61.
10 *Ibid.*
11 *Ibid.*, p. 62.
12 E. Fromm (1968) *The Revolution of Hope. Towards a Humanized Technology*, New York: Harper and Row, p. 137.
13 E. Fromm (2001) *op. cit.*, p. 31.
14 E. Fromm (2001) *The Fear of Freedom*, Abingdon: Routledge Classics, p. 121 ff.
15 *Ibid.*, p. 51.
16 E. Fromm (2001) *op. cit.*, p. 88.
17 R. Stevens (2008) *Erik H. Erikson: Explorer of Identity and the Life-Cycle*, Basingstoke: Palgrave Macmillan, p. 86.
18 E. Fromm (2001) *op. cit.*, p. 72.
19 *Ibid.*, p. 71. Fromm cites as his sources *Römerbrief*, 13, I and 'Against the Robbing and Murdering Hordes of Peasants' (1525): *Works of Martin Luther*, trans. C. M. Jacobs. A. T. Holman Company, Philadelphia, 1931, Vol. X, IV, p. 411.
20 R. Stevens (2008) *op. cit.*, p. 83.
21 *Ibid.*, p. 110.
22 *Ibid.*, p. 96.
23 *Ibid.*, p. 256.
24 R. Funk (2000) *op. cit.*, p. 74.
25 E. Fromm (1980b) *Arbeiter und Angestellte am Vorabend des Dritten Reiches. Eine sozialpsychologische Untersuchung*, Stuttgart: Deutsche Verlags-Anstalt, pp. 294–300.
26 E. Fromm (1999) *GA III Empirische Untersuchungen zum Gesellschafts-Charakter* (1936 'Autorität und Familie. Geschichte und Methoden der Erhebungen'), pp. 225–230.
27 W. Bonss (1980) 'Kritische Theorie und empirische Sozialforschung: Anmerkungen zu einem Fallbeispiel', in: E. Fromm (1980b) *op. cit.*, pp. 7–46.
28 R. Funk (2000) *op. cit.*, p. 90.
29 E. Fromm (1999) *GA III, op. cit.* (1970 'Social Character in a Mexican Village. A Sociopsychoanalytic Study', German trans. Liselotte and Ernst Mickel), p. 267.
30 E. Fromm (1980b) *op. cit.*, p. 52.
31 R. Funk (2000) *op. cit.*, p. 145.
32 D. Burston (1991) *The Legacy of Erich Fromm*, Cambridge (Mass.) and London: Harvard University Press, p. 27.
33 E. Fromm (2002) *op. cit.*, p. 352.
34 *Ibid.*
35 *Ibid.*, p. 6.
36 E. Fromm (1968) *op. cit.*, p. 39.
37 E. Fromm (2002) *op. cit.*, p. 105.
38 E. Fromm (2001) *op. cit.*, p. 96.
39 E. Fromm (2002) *op. cit.*, p. 107.
40 E. Fromm (2001) *op. cit.*, p. 91.
41 E. Fromm (2002) *op. cit.*, p. 180.
42 H. A. Jack (1987) Die Friedensbewegung und Erich Fromm Erstveröffentlichung in: Lutz von Werder (ed.) *Der unbekannte Fromm. Biographische Studien (Forschungen zu Erich Fromm*, Band 2, Haag und Herchen: Frankfurt, pp. 61–69 (trans. Petra Tauscher) (Fromm Archive).
43 E. Fromm (2002) *op. cit.*, p. 7.
44 E. Fromm (2002) *op. cit.*, p. 10.

45 https://www.cia.gov/library/publications/the-world-factbook/rankorder/2004
    rank.html, accessed 18/6/08.
46 http://www.who.int/mental_health/prevention/suicide/suiciderates/en/, accessed
    18/6/08.
47 *Ibid.*, p. 349.
48 E. Fromm (2002) *op. cit.*, p. 269.
49 E. Fromm (1980a) *op. cit.*, p. 170.
50 E. Fromm (1968) *op. cit.*, p. 94.
51 E. Fromm (2002) *op. cit.*, p. 353.
52 *Ibid.*, p. 255.
53 For more details on Owen's ideas, see I. Donnachie (2000) *Robert Owen: Owen of
    New Lanark and New Harmony*, East Linton: Tuckwell Press.
54 E. Fromm (2002) *op. cit.*, p. 276.
55 *Ibid.*, p. 293.
56 *Ibid.*, p. 331.
57 E. Fromm (1968) *op. cit.*, p. 95.
58 E. Fromm (1999) *GA V Politik und sozialistische Gesellschaftskritik* (1966 'Psycho-
    logical Aspects of the Guaranteed Income', German trans. Liselotte and Ernst
    Mickel), pp. 309–316.
59 E. Fromm (1979) *To Have or To Be?*, London: Abacus, p. 173.
60 *Ibid.*, p. 176.
61 *Ibid.*, p. 189.
62 E. Fromm (2002) *op. cit.*, p. 17.
63 E. Fromm (1968) *op. cit.*, p. 100.
64 E. Fromm (1979) *op. cit.*, p. 178.
65 E. Fromm (1968) *op. cit.*, p. 116.
66 E. Fromm (2002) *op. cit.*, p. 334.
67 *Ibid.*, p. 335.
68 E. Fromm (1980a) *op. cit.*, p. 169.
69 E. Fromm (1979) *op. cit.*, p. 184.
70 *Ibid.*
71 E. Fromm (1979) *op. cit.*, p. 185.
72 E. Fromm (1980a) *op. cit.*, p. 163.
73 E. Fromm (1975) *The Art of Loving*, London: Unwin Paperbacks, p. 70.
74 *Ibid.*, p. 343.
75 R. Dawkins (2007) *The God Delusion*, London: Black Swan Transworld
    Publishers.
76 R. Dawkins (2007) *op. cit.*, p. 389.
77 E. Fromm (2002) *op. cit.*, pp. 335–336.
78 R. Funk, Personal communication, July 2006.
79 E. Fromm (1999) *Erich Fromm Gesamtausgabe in zwölf Bänden* (ed. R. Funk) *Band VI
    Religion* (1965 'Preface to "Rumi the Persian"', German trans. Liselotte and Ernst
    Mickel), Stuttgart: Deutsche Verlags-Anstalt, p. 358.
80 *Fromm Forum Sonderheft* 11a/2007 Erich Fromm und der Dialog der Kulturen.
    Tübingen: Internationale Erich-Fromm-Gesellschaft.
81 The Universal House of Justice (1986) *The Promise of World Peace*, London: One
    World Publications, p. 35.
82 E. Fromm (1975) *op. cit.*, p. 70.
83 B. Landis (2008) 'When You Hear the Word, the Reality Is Lost', in: R. Funk (2009)
    (ed.) *The Clinical Erich Fromm. Personal Accounts and Papers on Therapeutic
    Technique*, Amsterdam-New York: Rodopi.
84 E. Fromm (1980a) *op. cit.*, p. 166.
85 E. Fromm (2002) *op. cit.*, p. 344.

86 See for example G. Pearson (1983) *Hooligan*, London: Macmillan.
87 E. Fromm (2002) *op. cit.*, p. 12.
88 *Ibid.*, p. 13.
89 See for example: http://www.nesta.org.uk/assets/Uploads/pdf/Provocation/market_failure_provocation_NESTA.pdf, accessed 1/12/08.
90 D. Ingleby (1991) 'Introduction', in: E. Fromm (2002) *The Sane Society*, London: Routledge Classics, p. xliii.
91 E. Fromm (1979) *op. cit.*, p. 196.
92 *Ibid.*

Chapter 6

1   D. Ingleby (1991) 'Introduction', in: E. Fromm (2002) *The Sane Society*, London: Routledge Classics, p. lii.
2   D. E. Schecter (1981 and 1958) 'To Be Truly with Him One Felt Fully Alive and Awake', in: R. Funk (2009) (ed.) *The Clinical Erich Fromm. Personal Accounts and Papers on Therapeutic Technique*, Amsterdam-New York: Rodopi.
3   E. Fromm (1999). *Erich Fromm Gesamtausgabe in zwölf Bänden* (ed. R. Funk) *Band XI Politische Psychoanalyse, Schriften aus dem Nachlass*, Stuttgart: Deutsche Verlags-Anstalt (1974 'Im Namen des Lebens', Radio Interview with Hans Jürgen Schultz), p. 617.
4   E. Fromm (1999) *GA XI, op. cit.* (1968 'Reconciliation in Our Nation' – Fromm wrote this as an election speech for Eugene McCarthy, German trans. Rainer Funk), p. 588.
5   E. Fromm (1980*) Beyond the Chains of Illusion. My Encounter with Marx and Freud*, London: Abacus, p. 3.
6   E. Fromm (1999) *GA XI, op. cit.*, Rainer Funk's commentary, p. 665.
7   E. Fromm (1980) *op. cit.*, p. 5.
8   *Ibid.*, p. 17.
9   E. Fromm (2001) *The Fear of Freedom*, Abingdon: Routledge Classics, p. 6.
10 E. Fromm (1979) *To Have or To Be?*, London: Abacus, p. 25.
11 R. Funk (1983) *Erich Fromm. Mit Selbstzeugnissen und Bilddokumenten*, Rororo Bildmonographie 322. Reinbek: Rowohlt Taschenbuch Verlag, p. 128.
12 A. Gourevitch (1981) ' I Always Felt Elated and Fortified', in: R. Funk (2009) *op. cit.*
13 E. Fromm (1980) *op. cit.*, p. 25.
14 R. Stevens (2008) *Freud: Shaper of the Unconscious Mind*, Basingstoke: Palgrave Macmillan, p. 155.
15 See for example R. Stevens (2008) *op. cit.*
16 E. Fromm (1980) *op. cit.*, p. 25.
17 E. Fromm (1999) *GA VI Religion* (1960 'Psychoanalysis and Zen Buddhism' and Rainer Funk's commentary, German trans. Marion Steipe with Rainer Funk), p. 378.
18 *Ibid.*, p. 341.
19 *Ibid.*, p. 352.
20 *Ibid.*, p. 356.
21 R. Funk (1982) *The Courage to Be Human* (trans. M. Shaw), New York: Continuum, p. 127.
22 R. Stevens (2008) *op. cit.*, p. 155.

23 E. Fromm (1999) *GA XII Psychoanalyse und Kunst des Lebens, Schriften aus dem Nachlass* (1974 'Meister Eckhart and Karl Marx on Having and Being', German trans. R. Funk), pp. 523–524.
24 *Ibid.*
25 E. Fromm (1979) *op. cit.*, p. 69.
26 A. Chaudhuri (1991) *Man and Society in Erich Fromm*, Delhi: Ajanta Publications, p. 209.
27 E. Fromm (1979) *op. cit.*, p. 25.
28 *Ibid.*, p. 47.
29 D. Ingleby (1991) *op. cit.*, p. xliii.
30 E. Fromm (1997) *The Anatomy of Human Destructiveness*, London: Pimlico, p. 40.
31 M. Bacciagaluppi (1989) 'Erich Fromm's Views on Psychoanalytic "Technique"', *Contemporary Psychoanalysis*, Vol. 25, No. 2 (Fromm Archive).
32 R. Biancoli (2006) 'The Search for Identity in the Being Mode', *Fromm Forum* 10/2006, Tübingen: International Erich Fromm Society, pp. 23–30.
33 E. Fromm (2005) Violence and its Alternatives. An Interview with F. W. Roevecamp (1968), *Fromm Forum* 9/2005, Tübingen: International Erich Fromm Society, p. 32.
34 Memories of Participants at the Ascona Meeting April 4–5, 1997 on 'Erich Fromm as a Psychoanalyst and Supervisor' (Fromm Archive).
35 D. Burston (1991) *The Legacy of Erich Fromm*, Cambridge (Mass.) and London: Harvard University Press, p. 1.
36 W. Hollway and T. Jefferson (2005) 'Panic and Perjury: A Psychosocial Exploration of Agency', *British Journal of Social Psychology*, 2005, 44, Issue 2, pp. 147–163.
37 E. Fromm (1997) *op. cit.*, pp. 79–80.
38 G. Chrzanowski (1997) 'Erich Fromm's Escape from Sigmund Freud: An Introduction to "Escape from Freedom"', *International Forum of Psychoanalysis*, 6, 3, pp. 185–189.
39 See for example F. Toates (2009) *Burrhus F. Skinner: Shaper of Behaviour*, Basingstoke: Palgrave Macmillan.
40 E. Fromm (1997) *op. cit.*, p. 71.
41 *Ibid.*, p. 73.
42 *Ibid.*, p. 78.
43 See for example P. Lunt (2009) *Stanley Milgram*, Basingstoke: Palgrave Macmillan.
44 E. Fromm (1997) *op. cit.*, p. 97.
45 M. Billig (1996) *Arguing and Thinking. A Rhetorical Approach to Social Psychology*. New edition. Cambridge: Cambridge University Press, p. 37.
46 E. Fromm (1997) *op. cit.*, p. 318.
47 *Ibid.*, p. 79.
48 E. Fromm (1975) *The Art of Loving*, London: Unwin Paperbacks, p. 33.
49 R. Frie (2003) 'Erich Fromm and Contemporary Psychoanalysis: From Modernism to Postmodernism', *The Psychoanalytic Review*, Vol. 90, No. 6, pp. 855–868 (Fromm Archive).
50 *Ibid.*
51 C. Rogers (1965) *Client-Centered Therapy*, Boston: Houghton Mifflin Company, p. 290.
52 E. Fromm (1997) *op. cit.*, p. 299.
53 E. Fromm (1999) *GA XII, op. cit.* (1989 'The Art of Being', German trans. Gisela Haselbacher and Rainer Funk), pp. 393–484.
54 *Ibid.*, (Rainer Funk's commentary), p. 548.
55 *Ibid.*, p. 438.
56 D. E. Schecter (1981 and 1958) *op. cit.*
57 E. Fromm (1968) *op. cit.*, p. 75.

58 E. Fromm (2001) *op. cit.*, p. 11.
59 E. Fromm (1968) *op. cit.*, p. 95.
60 R. Stevens (2008) *op. cit.*
61 A. Damasio (2000) *The Feeling of What Happens*, London: Vintage.
62 S. Zeki (2009) *Splendours and Miseries of the Brain. Love, Creativity and the Quest for Human Happiness*, Chichester: Wiley-Blackwell.
63 See for example S. Hanscomb (2006) 'Contemporary Existentialist Tendencies in Psychology', in: P. D. Ashworth and M. Cheung Chung (eds) *Phenomenology and Psychological Science. Historical and Philosophical Perspectives*, New York: Springer.
64 See for example M. Mair (1989) *Between Psychology and Psychotherapy: A Poetics of Experience*, London: Routledge.
65 D. Ingleby (1991) *op. cit.*, p. li.

Chapter 7

1   See for example http://www.esrcsocietytoday.ac.uk/ESRCInfoCentre/facts/UK/index51.aspx?ComponentId=12699&SourcePageId=18134, accessed 21/11/08.
2   L. Wilde (2004) *Erich Fromm and The Quest for Solidarity*, New York: Palgrave Macmillan, p. 4.
3   L. Wilde (2004) *op. cit.*, p. 44.
4   E. Fromm (2005) Violence and its Alternatives. An Interview with Frederick W. Roevekamp (1968), *Fromm Forum 9*, 2005, Tübingen: International Erich Fromm Society, p. 31.
5   R. M. Ryan and E. L. Deci (2002) 'Overview of Self-Determination Theory: An Organismic Dialectical Perspective', in: E. L. Deci and R. M. Ryan (eds) *Handbook of Self Determination Research*, Rochester: The University of Rochester Press, p. 7f.
6   E. Fromm (2005) *op. cit.*, p. 37.
7   See for example C. Peterson, S. F. Maier and M. E. P. Seligman (1993) *Learned Helplessness: A Theory for the Age of Personal Control*, New York: Oxford University Press.
8   M. E. P. Seligman (2003) *Authentic Happiness, Using the New Positive Psychology to Realize Your Potential for Deep Fulfillment*, London: Nicholas Brealey Publishing, pp. 132–133.
9   See for example R. Layard, (2006) *Happiness. Lessons from a New Science*, Harmondsworth: Penguin.
10 http://www.guardian.co.uk/commentisfree/2007/feb/20/wantedanerichfromm-party, accessed 21/11/08.
11 R. Layard, J. Dunn and the panel of the Good Childhood Enquiry (2009) *A Good Childhood. Searching for Values in a Competitive Age*, London: Penguin.
12 J. Cromby, B. Diamond, P. Kelly, P. Moloney, P. Priest and D. Smail (2007) 'Questioning the Science and Politics of Happiness', *The Psychologist*, 20, 7 p. 425.
13 See for example O. James (1998) *Britain on the Couch*, London: Arrow and O. James (2007) *Affluenza*, Vermilion: Random House Group.
14 O. James (1998) *op. cit.*, p. xi.
15 E. Fromm (2005) *op. cit.*, p. 33.
16 O. James (2007) *op. cit.*
17 E. Fromm (2005) *op. cit*, p. 33.
18 E. Fromm (2005) *op. cit.*, p. 36.
19 E. Fromm (1999) *GA XI Politische Psychoanalyse, Schriften aus dem Nachlass* (1974 'Im Namen des Lebens' Interview with Hans Jürgen Schultz), p. 612 ff.

20 http://www.statistics.gov.uk/CCI/nugget.asp?ID=1659&Pos=4&ColRank=2&Rank= 192, accessed 21/11/08.
21 E. Fromm (1997) *The Anatomy of Human Destructiveness*, London: Pimlico, p. 273.
22 See for example H. Dittmar (2004) 'Are You What You Have?', *The Psychologist*, April 2004, 17, 4, pp. 206–210.
23 E. Fromm (1979) *To Have or To Be?*, London: Abacus, pp. 93–94.
24 E. Fromm (1968) *The Revolution of Hope. Towards a Humanized Technology*, New York: Harper & Row, p. 12.
25 E. Fromm (1980) *Beyond the Chains of Illusion. My Encounter with Marx and Freud*, London: Abacus, p. 166.
26 K. J. Gergen (1991) *The Saturated Self: Dilemmas and Identity in Contemporary Life*, New York: Basic Books.
27 B. Schwartz (2004) *The Paradox of Choice: Why More is Less*, New York: HarperCollins.
28 R. Funk (2008) 'Entfremdung heute: Zur gegenwärtigen Gesellschafts-Orientierung', *Fromm Forum* 12/2008, Tübingen: International Erich Fromm Society, p. 64.
29 R. Robyn (2005) 'Introduction: National versus Supranational Identity in Europe', *The Changing Face of European Identity – A Seven-Nation Study of (Supra)National Attachments*, Abingdon: Routledge, p. 6.
30 *Ibid.*
31 See for example M. Argyle (2001) *The Psychology of Happiness*, Hove: Routledge.
32 http://www.guardian.co.uk/commentisfree/2007/dec/14/frommmetoyou, accessed 21/11/08.
33 See for example G. Egan (2007) *The Skilled Helper: A Problem-Management and Opportunity-Development Approach to Helping*, Eighth edition, Belmont: Thomson Higher Education.
34 See for example R. Gilligan (2000) *Promoting Resilience*, London: BAAF or G. Schofield (2001) 'Resilience and Family Placement: A Lifespan Perspective', *Adoption & Fostering*, 25, 3, pp. 6–19.
35 H. Wehr (2000) 'Biophile Alternativen in der Weiterentwickling der Schule', in: R. Funk, H. Johach and G. Meyer (eds) *Erich Fromm heute: Zur Aktualität seines Denkens*, München: Deutscher Taschenbuch Verlag, p. 118.
36 E. Fromm (1968) *op. cit.*, p. 36.
37 E. Fromm (1980) *op. cit.*, p. 167.
38 E. Fromm (2002) *The Sane Society*, Abingdon: Routledge Classics, p. 338.
39 O. James (1998) *op. cit.*, p. 70.
40 E. Fromm (2001) *op. cit.*, p. 102.
41 R. D. Putnam (1996: 56) cited in T. Schuller, S. Baron and J. Field (2000) 'Social Capital: A Review and Critique in Baron, Field and Schuller (2000)', *Social Capital: Critical Perspectives*, New York: Oxford University Press, p. 9.
42 R. D. Putnam (2000) *Bowling Alone. The Collapse and Revival of American Community*, New York: Simon and Schuster Paperbacks, p. 402.
43 E. Fromm (1999) *GA III Empirische Untersuchungen zum Gesellschafts-Charakter* (1970 E. Fromm and M. Maccoby 'Social Character in a Mexican Village. A Sociopsychoanalytic Study', German trans. Liselotte and Ernst Mickel), p. 271.
44 E. Fromm (1979) *op. cit.*, p. 19.
45 E. Fromm (2001) *op. cit.*, p. 112.
46 L. Wilde (2000) *op. cit.*, p. 50.
47 E. Fromm (1979) *op. cit.*, p. 17.
48 *Ibid.*, p. 19.
49 *Ibid.*
50 *Ibid.*, p. 44.
51 E. Fromm (2005) 'Do We Still Love Life' (first published in 1967), *Fromm Forum* 9/2005, Tübingen: International Erich Fromm Society, p. 11.

Index

Bold numbers indicate pages on which a topic or name is discussed in more depth.
Italics designate entries in *References and Notes*.